LLOYD CARR'S MICHIGAN FOOTBALL JOURNEY

How an Interim Coach Stepped Up for the Michigan Wolverines and Won His Way into the College Football Hall of Fame

Barry Gallagher

Power Group Publishing

Aurora, Illinois

Copyright © 2023 by Barry Gallagher

All rights reserved. No part of this publication may be reproduced, distributed, or transmitted in any form or by any means, including photocopying, recording, or other electronic or mechanical methods, without the prior written permission of the publisher, except in the case of brief quotations embodied in critical reviews and certain other noncommercial uses permitted by copyright law. For permission requests, write to the publisher, addressed "Attention: Permissions Coordinator," at the address below.

Barry Gallagher/Power Group Publishing
2748 Kirk Road, Suite 106, #298
Aurora, Illinois 60502
www.PowerGroup@comcast.net
Book Layout ©2017 BookDesignTemplates.com

Ordering Information:
Quantity sales. Special discounts are available on quantity purchases by corporations, associations, and others. For details, contact the "Special Sales Department" at the address above.

Lloyd Carr's Michigan Football Journey/Barry Gallagher —1st ed.

ISBN: 9798851945243

Sports/Coaching/Football (American)

TABLE OF CONTENTS

CHAPTER 1 Life Before Coaching at Michigan 1945 to 1980 1
CHAPTER 2 Carr Excels as a Michigan Assistant 1980 to 1994 13
CHAPTER 3 Intrim Coach Carr Steps Up 1995 23
CHAPTER 4 Looking to Improve 1996 33
CHAPTER 5 Let's Go Mountain Climbing! 1997 39
CHAPTER 6 How About an Encorc? 1998 49
CHAPTER 7 How About a Big Ten Threepeat? 1999 55
CHAPTER 8 Carr Leads Michigan into the Future 2000 61
CHAPTER 9 Was Coach Carr Feeling Lucky? 2001 69
CHAPTER 10 Time for Another Championship? 2002 73
CHAPTER 11 Another Championship Season 2003 79
CHAPTER 12 Ten Years in the Big Ten 2004 85
CHAPTER 13 Carr's Most Challenging Season 2005 91
CHAPTER 14 Carr's Wolverines Bounce Back 2006 95
CHAPTER 15 Lloyd Carr's Final Season 2007 101
CHAPTER 16 Coach Carr vs. the Nation 109
CHAPTER 17 Coach Carr vs. the Big Ten 119
CHAPTER 18 Coach Carr vs. Notre Dme 133
CHAPTER 19 Coach Carr vs. Minnesota 141
CHAPTER 20 Coach Carr vs. Ohio State 147
CHAPTER 21 Coach Carr vs. Michigan State 153
CHAPTER 22 Coach Carr and Michigan Stadium 165
CHAPTER 23 Lloyd Carr's Michigan Legacy 173

DEDICATION

*This book is dedicated to the memory of Chad Carr, beloved grandson of Coach Lloyd H. Carr Jr.
May Chad Carr Rest In Eternal Peace.*

A portion of the proceeds from the sale of this book will be donated by the author to the Chad Tough-Defeat DIPG Foundation.

Barry Gallagher

Foreword

(Note-Rich Hewlett earned four letters at Michigan-two as a quarterback and two as a defensive back. Defensive Backs Coach Lloyd Carr became Rich's position coach in 1981. They have been great friends ever since!)

Author Barry Gallagher chronicles Coach Lloyd Carr's legendary career at Michigan, detailing the great wins and tough losses, the rivalries, and, ultimately, his induction into College Football's Hall of Fame. Clearly, Lloyd was a highly successful football coach, and his record as Michigan's head coach places him only behind Fielding Yost and Bo Schembechler. What made him special though was everything else he brought to Michigan football and the University.

Coach Bo Schembechler hired Lloyd in 1980 to coach the defensive backs. He took over for Jack Harbaugh, one of Bo's renowned position coaches. Lloyd was young and aggressive, and possessed tremendous energy and intensity. His compassion and empathy for his players was unmatched.

Lloyd was not handed anything. His first year as an interim head coach was filled with private challenges, intense scrutiny, and public doubt. Initially, he wasn't going to be considered for the head coach position. Even so, Lloyd was not deterred. It wasn't about him; it was always about the team. Lloyd demonstrated incredible poise, leadership, and grace that season and his team responded. He earned and deserved the head coaching position at the University of Michigan.

Born from this work ethic was one of Lloyd's greatest character traits: his will to compete. Lloyd's intensely competitive spirit separates him from virtually every other coach. His will to prepare, compete, and win was matched only by Coach Schembechler. Bo and Lloyd had the distinctive ability to motivate and lead young men under any circumstance or challenge. Both of them willed their teams to victory more than once. Lloyd's teams went into every game truly believing they would beat any opponent, and his record against highly rated teams reflected his extraordinary competitive will to win.

Most people never knew how much of himself Lloyd poured into the Michigan football program. It was personal to Lloyd, and every fiber in his body desired to be the best for his staff, players, and the program. Lloyd Carr gave everything he had to the football program and demanded a lot from those around him -- both on and off the field. Lloyd had the unique ability to bring out the best in people.

This accountability was pervasive in every aspect of Lloyd's life and coaching. He was a disciplinarian, but he stood by his players and they respected him for it. If a player's discipline involved 6 A.M. stadium workouts, Lloyd was there, opening up the stadium. As a player worked out, Lloyd would walk the stadium's field preparing for his day. I was fortunate to join him on some of those walks. As we talked about life and the day's goals and challenges, the sun would come up over the rim of the stadium. He really loved being in the stadium at that time—surrounded by the quiet and its rich history. His love and respect for Michigan stadium contributed to his incredible success while coaching in it.

As his head coaching career wore on, his burning desire to win another national championship fueled him. He continued to have great teams and tremendous wins. And like all of us experience in life, he had difficult losses. Not surprisingly, for someone with his competitive spirit, he carried the losses with him.

But for those who know Lloyd, he's never been defined by the wins and the losses. Lloyd has always been much more than that. He cares deeply for the university and football program and has those same feelings for his players and coaches. He is incredibly loyal to his players and continues to support them and their families. In their times of need and difficulty, he stands strongly for them. Many former players, including myself, have leaned heavily on Lloyd's shoulder. He loves and cares deeply for his family, all of whom bring him tremendous joy.

Lloyd is generous with his time and money to the University, women's athletics, and the hospital system, especially at the children's hospital and the cancer center. Lloyd is a man of gratitude and never seeks recognition or acclaim for these contributions.

Lloyd Carr is also an avid reader and he consumed all types of literature. During an off-season, his reading intensified. Lloyd was always looking for a theme or message that he believed would help motivate and educate his players. During fall camp, while other programs drowned in the "X's and O's" or practice film, Lloyd would share with his teams the key stories that he had read.

He loved stories of adventure and was fascinated by the acts of Lewis and Clarke, Ernest Shackleton of Antarctica fame, and, of course, those who met the challenges of climbing Mt. Everest. As author Barry Gallagher points out, Lloyd used the preparation, challenges, and mental toughness needed to climb Mt. Everest as an analogy to attack the 1997 schedule; rated the hardest schedule in college football. Lloyd also loved telling his friends about the best books he had read. He would make notes throughout his books and write out important messages and themes in the margins. He freely passes his books around to his friends and family and continues to do so today.

At his core, Lloyd was a teacher of football and life. Lloyd kept a giant Webster's dictionary just outside his office. Every player that came in to see him had to read through the dictionary and come up with a word or words and be prepared to know how it was used and discuss its meaning. Lloyd and his players had fun with that exercise. Lloyd also taught his players how to compete at an elite level, how to pick yourself up when you get knocked down, and how to deal with success and disappointment – on and off of the field. He taught them the importance of a will to succeed and how a strong will often defeats better talent. Lloyd showed humility and grace in victory and took full responsibility for the losses.

Lloyd believed, as did Bo, that the team is greater than its parts. Both of them instilled in their players a love for teamwork. Many of Lloyd's players still carry that ethos in their daily lives.

Above all, Lloyd is a fierce and loyal friend to many. He understood and shared that being a friend was different than other relationships. He knew that friends sacrificed for each other, reveled in the success of the other, and shared their joys and sorrows. Lloyd has been a true friend to many people, and to be his friend carries significant meaning.

Over the last 43 years, I've been blessed to have gone from being one of his players to one of his friends. It was an honor to play two years for Lloyd, but it's a privilege to be his friend. We've laughed together and cried together. We know each other better than most and have leaned on each other at many different points in our lives. We've shared incredible highs and suffered devasting loss. Now, when we see each other and say goodbye for the moment, we tell each other, "I love you." That to me, is the greatest honor you can have with your friend, and it epitomizes the man that is Lloyd Carr. Thanks for your love and friendship, Lloyd. To me, and to so many others.

Lastly, thank you to Barry Gallagher for doing something that is long overdue. I am grateful for Barry's work. I've known Barry for many years, since he first started to write about Coach Bo and Michigan football. Barry also stands for loyalty and integrity. This book about Lloyd and his accomplishments reflects Barry's sincere love and appreciation for Lloyd and Michigan. Thank you Barry for pouring your heart and soul into this book on Lloyd, and a special thank you for inviting me to write this Foreword.

Rich Hewlett
August 2023

Introduction

I first met Coach Lloyd Carr in 1986 in the old football offices that used to be in what is now called Weidenbach Hall. It was a short, impromptu encounter but I still remember it to this day.

I saw him again in January 1988, I was involved with a group of people who worked to get Phil Webb inducted into the Romeo High School Athletic Hall of Fame. Phil was recruited by Lloyd Carr. It was a close call between Michigan State and Michigan. Fortunately, Phil chose Michigan. He wore #46 and played for the Wolverines from 1984 to 1987. Coach Carr represented the Michigan football program at Phil's induction ceremony on a cold winter's night. Lloyd Carr spoke highly of Phil Webb's legacy at Romeo High School and his outstanding work at Michigan. It was obvious to everyone in attendance that Lloyd Carr knew Phil and cared about him deeply as a player and a person.

My final encounter with Lloyd Carr took place at the Big Ten Kickoff Luncheon in Chicago in July 2014. As always, he was gracious despite being sought out by many fans that day. I thanked him again for helping us honor Phil Webb in January 1988. I also told him that I respected his outstanding career and thanked him for doing such a great job at Michigan.

I always respected the way that Lloyd Carr coached and the way he treated his players. I appreciated his calm, focused demeanor. Coach Carr was a "players" coach who was adept at bringing out the best in his athletes. He proved to be an outstanding recruiter, motivator, and leader. Lloyd Carr was a master of glib, one line, comments when television reporters stuck their microphones in his face as he left the field at halftime. Lloyd H. Carr worked in the shadows of the great Michigan football coaches. By the time he retired, Coach Carr he had carved out a special place in Wolverine football history with his exceptional achievements on and off the football field.

As an avid Michigan football fan and author, I was always amazed that there was no book available about Coach Carr's accomplishments. He is the winningest football coach and the third winningest head coach at the winningest program in college football history. Lloyd Carr is the last Wolverine football coach to win a national championship. His 1997 team accomplished something that had not been done in nearly fifty years. Now, twenty-five years later, that feat has not been replicated by any Michigan football team. Winning a national championship is a really special achievement because it is so darned hard to do. He also won five Big Ten Championships along the way. Now that Coach Carr is a member of the College Football Hall of Fame, I knew I had to take matters into my own hands.

Fortunately, I was able to meet with Coach Carr prior to the publication of this book. I also visited a close friend of Lloyd's in Riverview, Michigan which was amazing. Originally, Coach Carr talked about meeting for lunch. However, I wondered how that was going to work since he is so revered in Ann Arbor. Instead, we met at the house. It was me, Coach Carr, and Parker the dog. It was what I call a "Forrest Gump Moment."

Coach Carr was mine for almost two hours. It didn't take long to discover that he is a wonderful person to talk with but a difficult person to interview. I came to Ann Arbor intent on discovering the family values and foundational experiences that were established when he graduated from Riverview High School in 1963. In short, I wanted to discover what made Coach Carr "tick." After the first few questions, he started asking me questions that were designed to discover what made me "tick." Hmmmm. It didn't take long to figure out that I was sitting in front of a master of respect and relationship building. Coach Carr answered all the questions that I asked but I ran out of time because I had to answer his as well. It all worked out in the end but I left wanting to know more. The good news was that I returned to Chicago with an even greater appreciation of Lloyd Carr. My trip and my visit validated my desire to share his story.

The purpose of this book is simple. I want to shine a very bright light on Lloyd Henry Carr Jr. and his amazing Michigan Wolverine football journey. This book is a story about a young man who graduated from high school with a goal of a "career in athletics." (Quote from his high school yearbook, see Page 5 of this book). As it turned out, Lloyd Carr exceeded his own expectations since he carved out a "Hall of Fame" coaching career at the University of Michigan.

I didn't ask Coach Carr if I could write this book because I figured he would say no. Lloyd Carr is not a man who seeks attention. He is a very private man who worked in a very public job for decades. This book won't tell you everything that you probably want to know about Coach Carr. However, it will tell you why his story is worth telling and reading.

I have felt for many years that Lloyd Carr deserved a book. Now, he has one! It's time to take a closer look at Coach Carr's inspiring work in Ann Arbor from 1995 to 2007. Go Pirates! and Go Blue!

Barry Gallagher
August 2023

Please note that I capitalize the "C" when I am talking about Coach Lloyd Carr. So many people have called him "Coach" for so many years that it is practically his second "first" name. Of course, he loves being called "Coach" so that's why I did it. Technically, it is not grammatically correct, but for this man and for this book, I think it's perfect!

Barry Gallagher

CHAPTER 1

Life Before Coaching at Michigan
1945 to 1980

Lloyd Henry Carr, Jr. was born on July 30, 1945 in Hawkins County, Tennessee. His loving parents, Lloyd Sr. and his mother Pauline, also had a daughter named Patricia who was older than Lloyd. When Carr was ten years old, the Carr family moved to Riverview, Michigan. Lloyd's father landed a job at the sprawling McClouth Steel Plant in Trenton, Michigan. Riverview is located about six miles south of Detroit. It was a typical suburb that was built by hard working men and women who labored in the steel mills, automobile plants, and other area businesses. If you look on the City of Riverview's website today, the city tagline reads, "A great place to live, work and play." It appears that Riverview has been a great place to live for thousands of residents over the years. I think it was a great place for the Carr Family too.

A Successful Athlete at Riverview High School

Lloyd Carr fell in love with sports at a young age. His favorite baseball player was Mickey Mantle when he lived in Tennessee. Then, he became a fan of a Detroit Tiger named Al Kaline. Detroit Lion quarterback Bobby Layne also became a Carr favorite after he landed in Riverview. The City of Riverview had all the youth sports opportunities that a young boy could possibly want.

Carr grew up to be an outstanding athlete at Riverview Community High School. He earned nine varsity letters since he was a three-sport athlete who played football, basketball, and baseball. He played on Riverview's Class B State Championship football team that led the state in scoring in 1961. Carr did not start as a sophomore on the varsity but he must have played a lot since the Pirates won every game by at least twenty-points except one. As a senior, Captain Lloyd Carr helped lead the Riverview Pirates to an undefeated season, a conference championship, and a #5 ranking in Class B football in 1963. He finished his football career as an All-State quarterback in Class B football for his outstanding play in 1962.

Lloyd Carr played on a lot of winning teams in Riverview. During his high school days, the Pirates won state championships in football and cross country. They also finished as the second-best Class B swimming team in 1963 by one-half point. (Ugh) The Pirates won league championships in basketball and baseball when Lloyd was in high school. Riverview also won a district championship in basketball during the "Carr Years" at RHS. Wow, Riverview was an athletic powerhouse! Guess what? Lloyd Henry Carr Jr. was voted the "Best Male Athlete" in his senior year at Riverview. Of course, this was quite an honor considering the quality of the athletic programs at Riverview High School. In addition to his athletic prowess, Carr demonstrated leadership since he served as the Junior Class President in 1961-1962.

Image 1: Yes, this picture of Senior football Captain Lloyd Carr is almost larger than life. However, in Lloyd Carr's case that is not the case. Photo courtesy of Riverview Community Schools, Riverview, Michigan.

Lloyd Carr's parents gave him all the love that they could give him. They helped him develop a tireless work ethic, a strong Christian faith, and a deep appreciation for education that served Lloyd well for his entire life. Carr's youth sports coaches taught him to practice hard and compete at a high level. His high school coaches had a huge impact on Carr, especially his varsity coaches since he played for each of them for three years.

A man named Owen McCourt seemed to have the most powerful impact during Lloyd Carr's high school years. McCourt was an English and History teacher at RHS. He was also the Head Football Coach of the Pirates. (Guess what? Lloyd Carr majored in English and minored in History in college. Of course, he also coached football. Are we starting to see a connection here?) The 1961 Pirate Yearbook was dedicated to Mr. McCourt. Here is what the yearbook staff wrote about Owen McCourt:

We gratefully dedicate our 1961 Pirate to Coach McCourt through whose rogish wit we have learned to enjoy life and whose devotion to duty has taught its purposefulness. You, Coach, are the undefeated master of the development of character as well as champions; sportsmanship as well as sports; and team spirit as well as fighting spirit. Win or lose, you have earned the respect of the students, teams, school, and citizens of Riverview. (Courtesy of Riverview Community Schools, Riverview High School Pirate Yearbook, 1961, Page 2)

This heartfelt dedication helped me understand the kind of teachers, coaches, and mentors that guided young people at Riverview High School in the decade of the 1960s and beyond. There is no doubt that thousands of students in Riverview had the opportunity to learn, grow, and dream big dreams—very big dreams in some cases. Lloyd Carr was one of those fortunate individuals. Go Pirates!

```
LLOYD HENRY CARR JR.

Football 9,10,11,12
     Captain 12
Basketball 9,10,11,12
Baseball 9,10,11,12
Varsity Club 10,11,12
Pirate Log 12
Class    President 11

Ambition:    Career  in
Athletics

Will: "my title of Reverend
on the football team to Skip
Fowkes"
```

Image 2: Lloyd Carr had a lot to smile about when he graduated from Riverview High School in 1963. He earned a football scholarship to the University of Missouri. I am sure he was eager to follow in the football footsteps of Wally Widenhofer and Bill McCartney who made their way to Columbia, Missouri before Lloyd Carr. Photo courtesy of Riverview Community Schools, Riverview, Michigan.

College Athlete at Missouri and Northern Michigan

Carr's outstanding credentials helped him earn a football scholarship to the University of Missouri. He played for Dan Devine's Tigers from 1963 to 1965. Missouri went 14-5-2 in Carr's last two seasons in Columbia. The only thing that Coach Carr mentioned about Missouri was that he was in the Army ROTC program. He also told me that he was in his ROTC class the hour/day that President Kennedy was shot in 1963. Lloyd Carr learned a few more things about discipline and leadership in his ROTC classes. Of course, he has a deep respect for the military and the people who serve our nation.

Lloyd Carr didn't play a lot as a Missouri Tiger. When assistant coach Rollie Dotsch left to take the head coaching job at Northern Michigan University, Carr followed him all the way to Marquette, Michigan. I am sure that his beloved mother packed him a warm coat and hat when he went north! Brrrr!

Image 3: Lloyd Carr wore #11 as a quarterback at Northern Michigan University in 1967. He started every game and helped lead the Wildcats to the first 9-0-0 regular season record in NMU football history. Permission: Northern Michigan University Sports Information Department.

Lloyd Carr had an opportunity to become a starting quarterback again. In those days, transfers had to sit out for a year. He learned his way around Marquette in 1966, went to practice, and started working on a Masters's Degree in Educational Leadership. In August 1967, he became the starting quarterback for the Northern Michigan Wildcats.

Lloyd Carr helped lead the Wildcats to a perfect regular season record of 9 wins and 0 losses. Unfortunately, Northern Michigan lost to Fairmont State in the NAIA semifinals and ended the season with a final record of 9 wins, 1 loss, and 0 ties.

Image 4: Lloyd Carr is pictured with the 1967 Northern Michigan University football team. He is seated in the first row, fourth man from the left. Permission: Northern Michigan University Sports Information Department.

The 1967 Northern Michigan University football team was the first Wildcat team to win nine games in a season. It was also the first Wildcat team to post an undefeated season of more than two games. The entire 1967 team now holds a spot in the Northern Michigan Hall of Fame for their outstanding season in 1967.

Lloyd Carr completed 52 of 99 passes for 642-yards in 1967. He also threw four touchdown passes. He guided the NMU offense to an average of 25.9 points per game. One of his favorite targets was a player named Jesse Jenkins who played with Carr at Riverview for two years.

Here is the season record for the Northern Michigan Wildcats in 1967.

1967 NMU Regular Season Record

Opponent	Result	Final Score
Northern Iowa	Won	7-3
Akron	Won	34-17
Bemidji State	Won	33-3
Central Michigan	Won	21-15
Hillsdale	Won	35-8
Marine Corps	Won	27-0
St. Norbert	Won	24-23
Mankato State	Won	45-0
North Dakota	Won	26-6
Totals	9-0	252-75

Yes, Lloyd H. Carr finished his college football career on a very positive note. He also left Marquette, Michigan with a Master of Arts in Educational Leadership. Now, he was ready to start his "real" career.

Carr Begins His Teaching and Coaching Career

After graduation, Lloyd Carr returned to the Detroit area to start his teaching and coaching career. He served as a teacher and assistant coach at Detroit Nativity High School from 1968 to 1969. Carr moved on to a four-year stint at Belleville High School in Belleville, Michigan from 1970 to 1973.

In 1973, Lloyd Carr took the head coaching job at John Glenn High School in Westland, Michigan. He rebuilt the program over the course of the next three seasons which culminated in an outstanding record of 8 wins and 1 loss in 1975. Coach Lloyd Carr earned Regional Coach of the Year Honors in 1975.

Somehow, in the midst of coaching and teaching English and History, Lloyd Carr also found time to do something else. Carr ran for a vacant position on the school board and won. At thirty years of age, he was already finding ways to impact the community that he loved so much. Lloyd Carr was able to juggle all of these responsibilities and move forward in his coaching career.

Lloyd Carr told me that he learned a lot about leadership while serving on the Riverview School Board. He became even more passionate about teaching, learning, and education, if that was even possible. He also learned about strategic leadership and the long-term effects of some important decisions. Yes, a leader has to have one foot in the present, but he/she also must have the other foot in the future if the organization is going to be ready for what is next. As a leader, Lloyd Carr was always thinking about the future.

Image 5: Defensive backs coach Lloyd Carr with some of his players at Eastern Michigan University in 1976. Permission: Eastern Michigan University Athletics

In 1976, Ed Chlebek, Eastern Michigan University's new head coach, made Lloyd Carr an offer that he couldn't refuse. Well, Lloyd could have refused it, but he didn't. Carr made a big decision and decided to become a full-time assistant football coach for the Hurons.

Things went badly for EMU in 1976 since the Hurons ended the season with a final record of 2 wins and 9 losses. Year two of the Chlebek Era went much better. The Hurons finished the season with a record of 8-3-0. Chlebek's success earned him a promotion to the job at Boston College. Lloyd Carr did not go to Boston with Ed Chlebek.

After Chlebek's departure, Lloyd Carr moved on to a new job at the University of Illinois in 1978. Carr's new boss was a guy named Moeller, Gary Moeller.

Of course, Moeller was an Ohio State grad who coached for Bo at Miami of Ohio for two years before moving to Ann Arbor when Bo took the head coaching job at Michigan. Moeller coached at Michigan from 1969 through the 1976 season. He was doing an excellent job as Bo's defensive coordinator. In fact, he was doing so well that the University of Illinois thought he would make an outstanding head coach. Bo recommended Moeller for the Illinois job. He believed that Gary would be able to turn the struggling Illini football program into a winning organization.

Things definitely did not work out at the University of Illinois for Coach "Mo" and his staff. Carr was only on the Illinois football staff for two seasons. The Fighting Illini struggled in 1978 and 1979 and posted a record of 3 wins, 16 losses and 3 ties. Unfortunately, those numbers were not good enough. So, Gary Moeller, Lloyd Carr, and everyone else on the Illinois football staff were all looking for a job in January 1980.

Lloyd Carr probably did not have any great memories from his two seasons in in Urbana-Champaign, Illinois.

Actually, I wanted to ask Coach Carr about his two years in Urbana-Champaign but we ran out of time. I am ninety-nine percent certain that his time at Illinois left a bad taste in his mouth. A taste that lingered for the rest of his coaching career. Lloyd Carr didn't know it at the time, but things would be better regarding Illinois in the future, but I don't think he liked being fired by the Fighting Illini. Actually, I think that experience always fired him up when Illinois showed up on a Michigan football schedule. I will write more about that later in the book.

As it turned out, Lloyd Carr found his way to Ann Arbor in August of 1980. The rest, as they say, is history!

CHAPTER 2

Lloyd Carr - Michigan Assistant Coach 1980 to 1994

Bo Schembechler didn't like the way that Illinois treated Gary Moeller. In fact, he felt that Coach Mo had the Fighting Illini football program headed in the right direction. In an unprecedented move, Bo hired Moeller back to coach his quarterbacks in 1980. It was the first, and only, time that Bo allowed a former assistant to return to his coaching staff.

Moeller Puts in a Good Word For Carr

Meanwhile, Lloyd Carr had a family to support, so he accepted a coaching job to coach defensive backs at West Virginia. The bad news is that he only lasted a few months before he left Don Nehlen's program. The good news is that Gary Moeller put in a good word for Carr and Bo hired him to coach defensive backs for the Wolverines. Lloyd Carr never looked back. He made Ann Arbor his home for the next forty plus years!

Lloyd Carr Proved to be a Valuable Assistant - 1980 to 1986

Lloyd Carr's first season at Michigan got off to a winning start since the Wolverines defeated Northwestern by a score of 17-10. It was a good way to begin the 1980 season since Bo's 1979 team ended the season with three straight losses. Game two did not go as well since Lloyd Carr's college coach at Missouri, Dan Devine, led his Notre Dame team to a 29-27 victory over the Wolverines in South Bend. Bo Schembechler was livid because his team had lost four of the last five games. He decided to scrap his old option offense and go to a more balanced attack that would showcase the arm of John Wangler, the legs of Butch Woolfolk, and the hands of Anthony Carter.

The Wolverines didn't get all the bugs worked out of their new offense and they lost to South Carolina by a score of 17-14. Then things really turned around in Ann Arbor. Michigan had a record of 1 win and 2 losses to start the season and never lost again in 1980. Yes, they won nine straight games that included three shutouts in the last four games of the season. The Wolverine defense did not allow a touchdown for the last four games of the season or in the Rose Bowl. Michigan defeated Washington (23-6) to win the 1981 Rose Bowl.

After seven straight bowl losses, Bo Schembechler finally won his first bowl game. Michigan defeated Washington (23-6) to win the 1981 Rose Bowl. The 1980 season got off to a rough start but Michigan finished strong with a final record of 10 wins and 2 losses, a Big Ten Championship, and a Rose Bowl Trophy.

Lloyd Carr impressed Bo with some outstanding work as defensive backs coach from 1981 to 1983. Carr proved to be a valuable member of Bo's staff with his ability to teach, coach, and develop his players. Coach Carr also proved to be an excellent recruiter for Coach Schembechler and Michigan. The Wolverines posted a winning season in 1981 (9 wins and 3 losses) but finished in a tie for third place in the Big Ten with a record of 6 wins and 3 losses.

The 1982 team didn't win as many games (8 wins and 4 losses) but tied for the Big Ten Championship with a record of 8 wins and 1 loss in conference play. Carr coached his first All-Big Ten player when defensive back Keith Bostic earned the honor. In 1983 Lloyd Carr had another All-Big Ten performer named Evan Cooper. The Wolverines posted a record of 9 wins and 3 losses and went 8-1-0 in Big Ten play. Unfortunately, their only conference loss was to hated Illinois who won the Big Ten Title with a perfect record of 9-0-0. Michigan finished in second place in conference play in 1983.

Carr remained a vital part of Bo's staff from 1984 until 1986. He was still developing solid defensive backfields and providing valuable input on Coach Moeller's defensive game plans. Despite everyone's hard work, the 1984 season was Bo's worst. Key injuries and some bad luck resulted in a final record of 6 wins and 6 losses. It was like a bad dream and everyone hoped that the 1985 season would be better. As it turned out 1985 season was one of Bo's best. Jim Harbaugh's broken arm healed nicely and he led a high-scoring offense that racked up 342 points which was a lot more than the Wolverines scored in 1984 (214 total). Brad Cochran had an outstanding season and became Carr's first All-American defensive back.

The Wolverines posted a final record of 10 wins, 1 loss, and 1 tie and finished as the #2 ranked team in the country after a big win over Nebraska in the Fiesta Bowl.

The 1986 season also went well for Michigan since they ended the season with a final record of 11 wins and 2 losses. They tied for the Big Ten Championship with a final record of 7 wins and 1 loss. Gary Moeller's defense finished first in scoring defense since they only allowed 6.3 points per game. Moeller's Maulers also finished second in the nation in total defense with only 263.3 yards allowed per game. Carr's secondary only allowed 153.0 passing yards per game which was good for 15th best in the nation.

Michigan's defenders led the Big Ten in all categories (scoring defense, rush yards allowed, passing yards allowed, and total defense) in 1986. Coach Carr had another All-American performer in his defensive backfield named Garland Rivers. It was a very good year in Ann Arbor.

Bo Promoted Coach Carr to Defensive Coordinator - 1987

People were starting to take notice of Lloyd Carr's outstanding work. One of them was Notre Dame's Lou Holtz. According to John Kryk, author of *"Natural Enemies: Major College Football's Oldest, Fiercest Rivalry—Michigan vs. Notre Dame,"* Holtz offered Carr a job as his defensive backs coach. (Kryk, Page 254.) As it turned out, Bo had other plans since he moved Gary Moeller from Defensive Coordinator to Offensive Coordinator. Then, Schembechler offered Carr the Defensive Coordinator's job and that was that!

Michigan's offense was inconsistent in 1987 and scored forty-eight points less than they did in 1986 (379 points down to 331 points). The good news was that Lloyd Carr's defense only allowed 172 points in 1987 compared to 203 points in 1986. Unfortunately, the Wolverines slipped to an overall record of 8 wins and 4 losses. Michigan finished in fourth place in the Big Ten with a final record of 5 wins and 3 losses.

Things went much better in 1988 and 1989. Carr's defenses played excellent football and so did Moeller's offense. The result was back-to-back Big Ten Championships for Bo and Michigan. The Wolverines posted a 9-2-1 record in 1988 and improved to 10 wins and 2 losses in 1989. As it turned out, Carr and Moeller were done working for Bo Schembechler since he hung up his whistle officially in January 1990.

There was a lot going on with Bo's staff in December 1989. Lloyd Carr interviewed for the vacant head coach position at Wisconsin. The bad news was that Notre Dame's Defensive Coordinator, Barry Alvarez, got the job.

The good news was that Lou Holtz offered Carr the Defensive Coordinator job that Alvarez vacated. (Kryk, Page 255.) The best news was that Bo had the best plan all along. Athletic Director Schembechler named Mo as his replacement and Moeller hired Carr to be his Defensive Coordinator. So that was the end of the monkey business about Carr going to Notre Dame. He was destined to be a "Michigan Man" for the rest of his life. He just didn't know in what capacity!

Michigan's Overall Performance from 1980 to 1989

Year	W-L-T	Scored/Avg.	Allowed/Avg.	Difference
1980	10-2-0	322/26.8	129/10.8	+16.0
1981	9-3-0	355/29.6	162/13.5	+13.3
1982	8-4-0	345/28.8	204/17.0	+11.8
1983	9-3-0	355/28.9	160/13.3	+16.3
1984	6-6-0	214/17.8	200/16.7	+1.1
1985	10-1-1	342/28.5	98/8.2	+20.3
1986	11-2-0	379/29.2	203/15.6	+13.6
1987	8-4-0	331/27.6	172/14.3	+13.3
1988	9-2-1	361/30.1	167/13.9	+16.2
1989	10-2-0	335/27.9	184/15.3	+12.6
Total	90-29-2	3339/27.6	1679/13.9	+13.7

Lloyd Carr had a lot to do with the impressive statistics that Michigan posted while he was an assistant on Bo's staff from 1980 to 1989. The chart on the previous page shows the wins and losses and the average points scored and allowed from 1980 to 1989. The "Difference" column clearly shows why Michigan won so may games (90) in the decade of the 1980s. Bo had a lot of excellent coaches who helped Michigan achieve these numbers and Lloyd Carr was one of them!

The chart below paints a clear picture of how Bo's Wolverines did in the Big Ten from 1980 to 1989. Once again, the numbers are outstanding. It is easy to understand why Michigan won four Big Ten Championships in the decade of the Eighties and tied for another one.

Of course, an incredible amount of hard work by players and coaches goes into all of the numbers displayed below. Again, Coach Lloyd Carr was one of the talented and dedicated coaches who helped make these numbers happen!

Michigan's Big Ten Performance from 1980 to 1989

Year*	Place	W-L-T	Scored/Avg.	Allowed/Avg.	Difference
1980	1st	8-0-0	322/26.8	129/10.8	+16.0
1981	3rd(T)	6-3-0	355/29.6	162/13.5	+13.3
1982	1st	8-1-0	345/28.8	204/17.0	+11.8
1983	2nd	8-1-0	355/28.9	160/13.3	+16.3
1984	6th(T)	5-4-0	214/17.8	200/16.7	+1.1
1985	2nd	6-1-1	342/28.5	98/8.2	+20.3
1986	1st (T)	7-1-0	379/29.2	203/15.6	+13.6
1987	4th	5-3-0	331/27.6	172/14.3	+13.3
1988	1st	7-0-1	361/30.1	167/13.9	+16.2
1989	1st	8-0-0	335/27.9	184/15.3	+12.6
Total	--	68-14-2	2448/29.1	1041/12.4	+16.7

*Bold Year = Big Ten Championship Season

Coach Carr Gets Two Hats to Wear in 1990

Gary Moeller decided to give Lloyd Carr two jobs in 1990. Carr would be Michigan's Defensive Coordinator and also carry the additional title of Assistant Head Coach. Coach Mo was very aware that Lloyd had head coaching aspirations.

The title of Assistant Head Coach and Defensive Coordinator was Mo's way of helping Lloyd build his resume for future opportunities. Little did Moeller know that Carr's opportunity would come sooner than either man probably thought it would.

Lloyd Carr continued to serve Michigan and Gary Moeller well from 1990. The Wolverines won, or shared, three straight Big Ten Championships in Mo's first three seasons.

Once again, the numbers displayed below explain a lot about Michigan's football program from 1990 to 1994. The key statistics are very impressive from 1990 to 1993. Then, things slipped for Coach Moeller and his Wolverines in 1994. The chart below shows the wins and losses and the average points scored and allowed from 1990 to 1994. The two most important columns "W-L-T" and "Difference" column tell us everything we need to know about Michigan football in the Gary Moeller Era. Of course, Assistant Head Coach and Defensive Coordinator Lloyd Carr had a lot to say about these numbers—the good and the bad.

Michigan's Overall Performance from 1990 to 1994

Year	W-L-T	Scored/Avg.	Allowed/Avg.	Difference
1990	9-3-0	389/32.4	198/16.5	+15.9
1991	10-2-0	420/35.0	203/16.9	+18.1
1992	9-0-3	431/35.9	171/14.3	+21.6
1993	8-4-0	342/28.5	160/13.3	+15.2
1994	8-4-0	330/27.5	268/22.3	+5.2
Total	44-13-3	1912/31.9	1000/16.7	+15.2

Image 6: Lloyd Carr (right) is shown above with his friend and mentor Gary Moeller. They worked together for two years at the University of Illinois and fifteen more at Michigan before Moeller resigned in May 1995. Permission: Bentley Historical Library, University of Michigan.

Gary Moeller got off to a rough start in the Big Ten since he lost his first two games in 1990. Then, Michigan won thirteen straight games and remained undefeated in twenty-two straight games from late October 1990 to October 1993. Moeller's team defeated Iowa in the Big Ten opener in 1993. Michigan State ended Michigan's winning/undefeated ways in the second conference game of the 1993 season. Unfortunately, the Wolverine domination in the Big Ten ended with that bitter defeat in East Lansing.

Michigan's Big Ten Performance from 1990 to 1994

Year*	Place	W-L-T	Scored/Avg.	Allowed/Avg.	Difference
1990	1st (T)	6-2-0	247/30.8	135/16.8	+14.0
1991	1st	8-0-0	316/39.5	91/11.3	+28.2
1992	1st	6-0-2	280/35.0	113/14.1	+20.9
1993	4th (T)	5-3-0	194/24.2	91/11.3	+12.9
1994	3rd	5-3-0	220/27.5	177/22.1	+5.4
Total	--	30-8-2	1257/31.4	607/15.1	+16.3

*Bold Year = Big Ten Championship Season

The chart above paints a clear picture of how Mo's Wolverines did in the Big Ten from 1990 to 1994. Once again, the numbers from 1990 to 1992 are very impressive. It is easy to understand why Michigan won three straight Big Ten Championships to start the Moeller Era in Ann Arbor. Gary Moeller's offense averaged over thirty-points per game and Lloyd Carr's defenses were holding opponents to less than seventeen points, or less, per game. The result was point differentials that made Michigan hard to beat.

Things unraveled in 1993 and 1994, especially on offense. Coach Moeller's offense only averaged twenty-five points per game in the last two seasons. Lloyd Carr's defense was strong in 1993 and only allowed about eleven points per game. Unfortunately, Carr's defense went downhill in 1994 and allowed over twenty-two points per game. Michigan's point differential of +5.4 points was the worst since Bump Elliott's 1967 team posted a point differential of -3.5 points per game.

The biggest room in Schembechler Hall in January 1995 was the room for improvement. The Wolverines did not score enough points in 1994 and they allowed too many. Coach Moeller knew he had to turn things around in season number six. As it turned out, that did not happen.

CHAPTER 3

Interim Coach Carr Steps Up
Season One - 1995

Nobody in Wolverine Nation was happy about back-to-back seasons of 8 wins and 4 losses, especially Gary Moeller. Unfortunately, some of the natives were getting restless, but it did not matter since it appeared that Gary Moeller would be back for his sixth season in August 1995. All that changed in late April when Gary Moeller and some friends went out for dinner and drinks at a restaurant in Southfield, Michigan. Apparently, Moeller had too much to drink and made a big scene. A few days later, he resigned from one of the best coaching jobs in America.

Early May is generally not the time that most college programs go looking for a new football coach. Athletic Director Joe Roberson had to make the biggest decision of his tenure at a less than ideal moment. Because of the timing, looking outside the program was not possible. All of the best coaches were in place evaluating their spring football programs and getting ready for the fall camps that would start in a few short months. Mr. Roberson had a short list to work from, a really short list. It didn't take him long to figure out that he really only had one choice.

Gary Moeller was an easy choice for Bo to make in 1990 when it was time to choose his successor. Moeller had been at Michigan for a total of eighteen years out of a twenty-three coaching career. His only break in service was his first Head Coaching job at Illinois which lasted from 1977 to 1979. Moeller inherited a mess in Champaign. Just when it looked like things were heading in the right direction Illinois fired him at the end of the 1979 season. Moeller's firing also fired up a guy named Schembechler. Bo welcomed Mo back to Ann Arbor in a heartbeat and really enjoyed beating the school that gave Mo the shaft. Gary Moeller become Bo's top assistant having served him well as Defensive Coordinator and Offensive Coordinator and Assistant Head Coach. Bo was grooming Mo for bigger things and when Bo decided to retire—Mo was his man!

The circumstances were different this time. Michigan was in a tough spot and everybody knew it, especially Joe Roberson. Lloyd Carr was the Defensive Coordinator in 1994 and he also carried the title of Assistant Head Coach. Moeller respected Carr and he had become a loyal assistant who could coach, recruit, create game plans, you name it. He was a solid football man, a loyal Michigan man (Ten years for Bo and five for Mo), a man who knew the Michigan system that Bo created and Mo carried on. There were lots of plusses here, but he had only been a Head Coach for three high school seasons and that was twenty years ago. It's a pretty big jump from John Glenn High School to the University of Michigan. So, the question in Roberson's mind was "Could Lloyd Carr get the job done at Michigan?"

Image 7: Lloyd Henry Carr Jr. stepped up as "interim" head coach in May 1995. Thirteen years later he quietly won enough games and championships to qualify for entry into the College Football Hall of Fame. Permission: Bentley Historical Library, University of Michigan.

Again, Joe Roberson didn't have a lot of choices available to him. After exploring his very limited options he named Lloyd Carr's as the "interim" head coach. Mr. Roberson would wait and watch to see if Carr's could step up and lead the Wolverine Football program. The good news was that Michigan had a new football coach. Lloyd Carr would have a chance to prove that he was the right man for the job. The bad news was that nobody knew how long Carr's head coaching "tryout" would last.

Lloyd Carr presented himself well at his first press conference. He appeared confident, focused, and determined to make the best of a bad situation. He knew that no one in the Big Ten Conference was feeling sorry for Michigan. Of course, everybody in the Big Ten was probably hoping that Coach Carr would fall flat on his face. A few rough years in Ann arbor would make life a lot better for all Big Ten football coaches and athletic directors. Carr advised everyone who was listening "Don't shed any tears for Michigan…we will be back." Lloyd Carr passed his first press conference "test." Okay, maybe he would step up for Michigan football and be as successful as a head coach as he was as an assistant.

The Journey Begins

It didn't take long to find out if Lloyd Carr had what it took to lead the Michigan football program. His first season started off with his first game which was Michigan's first Pigskin Classic. This was the first nationally televised game of the 1995 season. It would also be the first game ever played in the month of August in the one hundred and sixteen-year history of Michigan Football. Lloyd Carr was making history in his first game as a Head Coach. It was about to get better, but not immediately.

Early in the fourth quarter, Carr's Wolverines were down by seventeen points. Things were not looking good for the young Wolverines and their "interim" coach. Coach Carr didn't panic and his players didn't either. His calm, but intense, demeanor helped his players remain focused and confident until they won on the last play of the game.

Team #116 – 1995   Record: 9 wins, 4 losses, and 0 ties

August 1995: 1 win and 0 losses

Image 8: Lloyd Carr faced off against George Welsh and his Virginia Cavaliers in August 1995. It may have been the hottest season opener in history of Michigan Stadium. Permission: Bentley Historical Library, University of Michigan.

Interim head coach Lloyd Carr was in complete command of the Michigan team in August 1995. His Wolverine coaching career began on a sweltering hot day in Ann Arbor on August 26, 1995. Carr was sweating it out the entire afternoon since it was so hot and also because his team was down by seventeen points at the start of the fourth quarter. The defense figured out how to stop Virginia and the Wolverine offense went to work. Finally, Scott Dreisbach threw a touchdown pass to Mercury Hayes for a last second 18-17 victory. Wow, what a start to the Lloyd Carr Era in Ann Arbor! Coach Carr's first Michigan victory was win #748 in Wolverine football history. So far, so good!

Image 9: Mercury Hayes caught the game winning touchdown that gave Coach Lloyd Carr his first victory in his first game at Michigan. It was an exciting start for Carr and his Wolverines thanks to that last second victory. Permission: Bentley Historical Library, University of Michigan.

Lloyd Carr earned his first head coaching victory in his first game as a college coach. It was the first time Michigan had ever overcome back a seventeen-point deficit and won the game. If you were counting, that was seven firsts in one game (first season for Carr, first game, first Pigskin Classic in U of M history, first game in August, first Carr victory, first game with over fifty Wolverine passes (52), and Michigan's first ever seventeen-point comeback win. It was very interesting when you think about it. There would be a lot more firsts to come in the Carr Era in Ann Arbor. One thing you can say about Lloyd Carr's career, it had a lot of highs, some awful lows, and some very, very interesting games.

I am going to use a consistent format for telling Coach Carr's story. First, I will give some background on each season of Coach Carr's tenure. Second, I will summarize the results from every month from all thirteen seasons. Third, I will share the results from all thirteen bowls games that the Wolverines played in from 1995 to 2007. Fourth, I will post a season summary that documents Michigan's final season record and how they fared in the Big Ten Conference competition. This section will also discuss player awards for each season. Finally, I will shift the focus from the team to Coach Carr and record any coaching milestones that Lloyd Carr earned along the way—and there were many!

September 1995: 4 wins and 0 losses

Things went even better the next week with a more convincing win over Illinois (38-14). Carr's footballers won three more games over Memphis (24-7), Boston College (23-13), and Miami of Ohio (38-19). The Lloyd Carr Era was off to a perfect start with 5 wins and 0 losses. His team was unranked at the start of the season but rose to #6 by the end of September.

October 1995: 2 wins and 1 loss

Coach Carr's first game against Northwestern did not go well. The underdog Wildcats were ranked (#25) and they had something to prove. Northwestern left town with an upset win (19-13) over the Wolverines. Michigan bounced back with wins over Indiana (34-17) and Minnesota (52-17) to remain in the Big Ten Title race. The Wolverines had a record of 7 wins and 1 loss heading into November.

November 1995: 2 wins and 2 losses

Unranked Michigan State, with a new coach named Nick Saban, came to Ann Arbor and left with a 28-25 win over seventh ranked Michigan. It was the first time that the Spartans and Wolverines faced off with rookie coaches since 1929. Carr's resilient team bounced back with an unusual 5-0 win over Purdue . That victory pushed Michigan to a record of 8 wins and 2 losses. It also resulted in the removal of "interim" from Carr's job title. Joe Paterno and Penn State showed no respect for Michigan's new head coach since they defeated Michigan in Happy Valley 27-17.

Coach Carr's Maize and Blue footballers had a ranking of #18 and a record of 8 wins and 3 losses heading into Ohio State week. How would his Wolverines do against John Cooper's highly ranked Buckeyes? Well, Michigan did just fine against OSU since Carr's eighteenth-ranked team upset # 2 Ohio State by a score of 31-23. It was one of the biggest upsets in the Michigan vs. Ohio State football series and one of the most surprising. It was a great way to finish Coach Carr's first regular season.

The win gave Michigan a record of 9 wins and 3 losses with one bowl game to go.

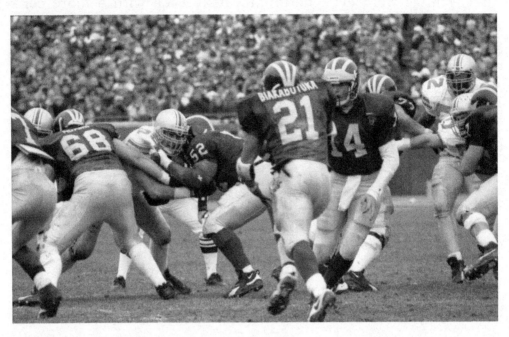

Image 10: Lloyd Carr figured out that his best play in the 1995 series game against Ohio State was a handoff from Brian Griese (#14) to Tim Biakabutuka (#21). This combination led to a record setting performance and a huge upset win for Michigan. Permission: Bentley Historical Library, University of Michigan.

Alamo Bowl: December 28, 1995 #19 Texas A&M 22 #14 Michigan 20

The fourteenth ranked Wolverines earned a spot in the Alamo Bowl against the nineteenth ranked Aggies from Texas A & M. The Aggies upset Michigan in a close game 22-20. It was a disappointing way to end a solid season that began with a lot of questions and uncertainty.

Season Summary:

The Wolverines finished with a final record of 9 wins and 4 losses which was one more win than Gary Moeller posted in 1994. Coach Carr's first team went 5-3-0 in the Big Ten and tied for third place. Lloyd Carr's job performance in 1995 clearly indicated that he had what it took to lead the Michigan football program. So far, so good!

Carr's Wolverines finished in the top twenty in both polls (#17 in the Associated Press poll and #19 in the CNN/USA poll).

Two Michigan stalwarts earned All-American honors in Coach Carr's first season in 1995. Guard Joe Marianaro and linebacker Jarrett Irons were recognized for their outstanding efforts during the season.

Irons and Marianaro earned All-Big Ten Honors along with offensive tackle Jon Runyan, center Rod Payne, and defensive backs Charles Woodson and Clarence Thompson.

Lloyd Carr's Coaching Milestones:

Yes, Lloyd Carr's first season at Michigan was memorable for many reasons. First, it was his first season as a head football coach at the college level.

Second, he earned his first win against Virginia in his first game.

Third, it was very fitting that he earned his first Big Ten victory against Illinois on September 2, 1995. I am certain that this one was special since Illinois fired Gary Moeller and Lloyd Carr and the rest of the staff in December 1979.

Fourth, Coach Carr sent the alumni home in a good mood since he won his first game against Minnesota (52-17) on October 28, 1995.

Fifth, "Interim" Coach Lloyd Carr earned his first shutout victory with a 5-0 win over Purdue in the Big House on November 11, 1995. The "Interim" part of his title was removed the next day when Athletic Director Joe Robeson figured out that Lloyd Henry Carr was the right man to lead the Michigan Football Program.

Sixth, Carr also posted his first win over a top ten opponent when his Wolverines defeated #2 Ohio State (31-23). Finally, Lloyd Carr posted his first nine-win season in 1995.

Finally, Lloyd Carr's first win at Michigan was also the 300th win in the history of Michigan Stadium.

All in all, it was an excellent start to what would become an outstanding career at Michigan. Lloyd Carr proved that he could lead and win as the head football coach in Ann Arbor.

CHAPTER 4

Looking to Improve Season Two - 1996

Michigan Head Coach Lloyd Carr impressed a lot of people with his debut season in 1995. His nine-win season was an improvement over the two straight eight-win seasons that Gary Moeller posted in his final two years in Ann Arbor. Unfortunately, he was coaching in Ann Arbor where winning is expected but eight and nine-win seasons are merely "tolerated." People in the Tree City really don't get too excited about a coach until he puts together two or three ten-win seasons or claims a Big Ten Championship. Carr knew he had some work to do if he wanted to remain in his current job. The good news was that he had some excellent players coming back and everyone expected that it would be another good season for Michigan. Many thought that his team could compete for the conference championship. After all, this was still Michigan, right?

Team #117 – 1996   **Record: 8 wins and 4 losses**

August 1996: 1 win and 0 losses

The Wolverines began the 1996 season as the twelfth ranked team in the country. For the second straight year, Michigan opened the season with an August game in Ann Arbor. And, for the first time in Wolverine football history, Michigan kicked off the season with a Big Ten game in August. The Wolverines played well and defeated Illinois by a score of 20-8.

Image 11: Scott Dreisbach used his arm and his legs in the season opening Big Ten win over Illinois in 1996. He scored Michigan's first touchdown on a 73-yard run and threw a 10-yard touchdown pass late in the game. Permission: Bentley Historical Library, University of Michigan.

September 1996: 3 wins and 0 losses

After a bye week, Coach Carr's team traveled to Colorado. The Wolverines returned with a 20-13 win over the fifth ranked Buffalos. Then, the #8 Wolverines defeated Boston College by the score of 20-14. Michigan hosted unranked UCLA on the last Saturday of September and sent the Bruins home to ponder a 38-9 defeat. Michigan rolled into October with a perfect record of 4 wins, 0 losses, and 0 ties. It was time to focus on winning a Big Ten Title.

October 1996: 2 wins and 1 loss

The Wolverines stepped into October on the wrong foot since they lost a 17-16 heartbreaker at Northwestern. They had an extra week to get ready for Indiana. The Homecoming Day crowd went home happy after a 27-20 Wolverine victory over the Hoosiers. Michigan finished the month of October on a strong note with a 44-10 win at Minnesota. Coach Carr's team was still in the hunt for a championship but they could not afford any slip ups in November.

November 1996: 2 wins and 2 losses

Michigan State came to town on November 2, 1996, and left Ann Arbor with a 45-29 loss. It was Carr's first win over MSU and Nick Saban's first loss to Michigan. The ninth ranked Wolverines traveled to West Lafayette, Indiana and lost a tough game to the Spoilermakers (9-3). Penn State showed up in the Big House and made it two losses in a row for Michigan since PSU won by a score of 29-17. Michigan did not appear to be ready for a trip to Columbus. However, they still had to show up and play #2 Ohio State.

For the second straight season, Lloyd Carr's Wolverines upset John Cooper and his second ranked Buckeyes. It was a close game but Michigan prevailed in Columbus (13-9). It was another satisfying win for the Maize and Blue footballers and another devastating loss for Ohio State. Of course, the two straight losses to Purdue and PSU knocked Michigan out of the conference title race. Michigan ended the regular season with a final record of 8 wins and 3 losses. Carr's team finished in a fifth-place tie in the Big Ten with a record of 5 wins and 3 losses. The good news was that they were going to play in the Outback Bowl. The bad news was that they had to play Alabama.

Outback Bowl: January 1, 1997 #16 Alabama 17 #15 Michigan 14

Michigan was favored to defeat the Crimson Tide, but it didn't play out that way. Michigan controlled the stats with 291-yards in the air and 181-yards on the ground. Alabama ran for 202-yards but only passed for 65-yards.

The difference in the game turned out to be a pick-six that a Crimson Tide defender returned 88-yards for the decisive points. The 17-14 defeat was another tough bowl loss for Coach Carr and his Wolverines.

Season Summary:

Season number two in the Lloyd Carr Era was full of high expectations, but two straight losses in November ended their Big Ten Title hopes. The good news was that Carr's Wolverines beat Ohio State for the second consecutive season. The bad news was that they did not win the Big Ten Championship in 1996. Another bowl loss ended the 1996 season on a sour note. Michigan's final record slipped to 8 wins and 4 losses. Unfortunately, that meant that the Wolverines posted four consecutive four loss seasons for the first time in program history.

Michigan closed the season as the twentieth ranked team in the nation in the Associated Press and the CNN/*USA Today* Coaches polls.

Four of Michigan's best players earned All-American honors in 1996. Center Rod Payne, linebacker Jarrett Irons, defensive tackle William Carr, and defensive back Charles Woodson were honored for their stellar play during the season.

In addition to the four men cited above, defensive end David Bowens, guard Damon Denson, safety Marcus Ray and tight end Jerame Tuman also earned All-Big Ten Honors.

The good news was that Coach Carr continued to prove that he was a solid leader. He was in control of himself and the Michigan Football program.

Of course, everyone in Ann Arbor was hoping for more in 1996. The big question in Ann Arbor was "Could Lloyd Carr lift the Michigan football team to greater heights?" Like every other coach, Carr was optimistic about the returning cast for the 1997 season. However, no one, not even Lloyd Carr, could have predicted what Michigan Football team number one hundred and eighteen was about to accomplish!

Lloyd Carr's Coaching Milestones:

Year two of Lloyd Carr's tenure had a few more milestones. First, Coach Carr earned his first rival road win over Minnesota with a 44-10 victory in Minneapolis on October 26, 1996.

Second, Coach Carr earned his first victory over Michigan State with a 45-29 victory in Ann Arbor on November 2, 1996.

Third, Carr posted his first win over the Buckeyes in Columbus thanks to a 13-9 upset over the #2 Buckeyes on November 23, 1996.

CHAPTER 5

Let's Go Mountain Climbing!
Season Three - 1997

The 1997 football season in Ann Arbor began with low expectations from many perspectives. The Wolverines had the toughest rated schedule in Division I-A football. The pre-season pollsters were not too fond of the Wolverines and only had them ranked number seventeen at the start of the season. They were picked to finish in the middle of the pack in the Big Ten because of an unsettled quarterback situation and lots of new faces on both sides of the ball. There was a solid core of experienced players, but way too many question marks. Lloyd Carr read an interesting book titled *Into Thin Air* by Jon Krakauer during the off-season. The book told the story about a failed attempt to scale Mount Everest. Carr recognized the difficulties of mountain climbing and how they related to the gauntlet of a long football season. He decided to use the mountain climbing metaphor to mentally prepare his Wolverines for the grueling eleven game season they were about to begin. Coach Carr had one of the survivors of the ill-fated climbing expedition, Lou Kasischke, speak to his Wolverines before the season started. His message really hit home with the Michigan football team in August 1997.

Coach Carr and his staff built on the "mountain climbing" theme starting with game one. The Michigan football staff used it to focus everyone's efforts on "one step and one game at a time." The synergy that was created by the mountain climbing analogy produced some stunning results!

The 1997 Michigan Football team was perfect—the first team in Michigan Football history to win twelve games and finish with no losses and no ties. Even though they won all of their games they were not as dominant as some Michigan teams of the past. They put up good numbers, consistent numbers, but outside of a couple blow out wins, not overwhelming numbers. They did not have a thousand-yard rusher or a receiver who even gained five hundred yards. What they did have was a balanced offensive attack led by a fifth-year senior Brian Griese. Michigan's stifling defense, led by Glen Steele and Charles Woodson, kept the Wolverines in every game.

Team #118 – 1997 ***Record: 12 wins and 0 losses***
Big Ten Champions & National Champions

September 1997: 3 wins and 0 losses

Under Coach Lloyd Carr's steady leadership, the Wolverines started their climb to the top of the college football mountain with a convincing 27-3 win over #8 Colorado. Then, the eighth ranked Maize and Blue footballers blasted unranked Baylor 38-3. Notre Dame came to the Big House with one goal—beat Michigan! The Fighting Irish led late in the game before the Wolverines prevailed by a score of 21-14. Michigan ended September as the sixth-ranked team in college football. Lloyd Carr's mountain climbing expedition was off to a good start!

October 1997: 4 wins and 0 losses

Michigan entered the conference schedule with a perfect record of three wins and no losses. Game four was a 37-0 blowout at Indiana. The Wolverines were climbing higher and higher and the air was starting to get a little thinner.

Northwestern was next on the schedule. They had beaten Coach Carr's in the last two games but the third game was not a charm for the Wildcats. The Wolverines sent their guests back to Evanston, Illinois with a 23-7 loss.

Game number six proved to be the toughest game of the season. The Wolverines trailed the visitors from Iowa 21-7 at halftime. Michigan game back to win by a score of 28-24. Whew, that was close! Coach Carr's Wolverines rose to number five in the polls as they continued their mountain climbing expedition. Michigan was perfect with a record of 6 wins and 0 losses. It was time for a trip to East Lansing for another battle for the Paul Bunyan Trophy and bragging rights for the Great Lakes state.

The number twenty-one ranked Spartans entered the game with six wins and one loss. Charles Woodson, and the rest of the defense, put on an incredible performance in East Lansing that included six interceptions (two for Woodson) for the Michigan defenders. This game also included Woodson's incredible leaping, one-handed, one leg in bounds interception that no one could believe.

MSU's record dropped to 6 wins and 2 losses after losing to Michigan 23-7. The Spartans and their fans watched the Paul Bunyan Trophy and their hopes for a Big Ten championship leave Spartan Stadium. He was a welcome guest on a rowdy Wolverine bus that was headed for Ann Arbor.

<u>November 1997</u>: 4 wins and 0 losses

By November 1st, everyone was starting to pay attention to the undefeated Wolverines (7 wins and 0 losses) for a lot of reasons. They were shutting down teams on defense and finding ways to win with a variety of offensive weapons. Woodson was starting to emerge as a big play threat since Coach Carr put him into more plays on offense. The Heisman talk started to become part of the college football conversation as the Wolverines continued their climb to gridiron glory.

Fourth ranked Michigan hosted a scrappy Minnesota team on Homecoming Day and sent them home with a twenty-one-point loss (24-3). This victory was noteworthy because it was Carr's twenty-fifth win as Michigan's head coach. Of course, he was just getting started. The next destination on the journey was Happy Valley where Joe Paterno's third ranked Penn State team was preparing to knock the Wolverines off the mountain.

What happened was quite the opposite. Michigan played their best game of the season and humbled the Nittany Lions by twenty-six points (34-8) and it wasn't even that close! The game proved to be the worst home loss in Joe Paterno's tenure at Penn State. Michigan dominated PSU in every phase of the game. Everyone, including the pollsters, took notice!

Michigan was the #1 team in the country the next week. The Wolverines won another difficult road game at Wisconsin (26-16) to push their record to 10 wins and 0 losses.

Image 12: Charles Woodson (#2) is on his way to a memorable punt return and a 78-yard touchdown against Ohio State in 1997. The win closed out a perfect regular season in 1997 and the punt return sealed the Heisman Trophy for Woodson. Permission: Bentley Historical Library, University of Michigan.

Ohio State came to town with one goal—topple the Wolverines. The Buckeyes put up a good fight but Michigan prevailed by a score of 20-14. Victory number eleven earned Lloyd Carr's first conference championship and a spot in the 1998 Rose Bowl. The Wolverines were almost to the top of the mountain. However, one big step remained!

Charles Woodson's phenomenal season was recognized and rewarded when he became the third Wolverine to win the Heisman Trophy in December 1997. He was the first three-way player (defender, special team star, and wide receiver) to be recognized as the player in college football.

Rose Bowl: January 1, 1998 #1 Michigan 21 #8 WSU 16

Lloyd Carr's "mountain climbers" had one more peak to conquer and that was at the 1998 Rose Bowl. The eighth ranked Washington State Cougars were the last obstacle that Lloyd Carr's Wolverines had to overcome. The first ever bowl game between Michigan (11-0-0) and Washington State (10-1-0) was a cliff-hanger all the way. Washington State scored first in the opening quarter. Ryan Leaf completed a 15-yard touchdown pass to Kevin McKenzie. Rian Lindell's extra point gave the Cougars a 7-0 lead after fifteen minutes of football. Michigan's offense woke up late in the second quarter. Brian Griese hit Tai Streets for a 53-yard score. Kraig Baker kicked the extra point and the game was tied at 7-7 at halftime. (Bentley Historical Library [BHL], Michigan's Bowl Game History, 1998 Rose Bowl, Page 1)

The Cougars drove 99-yards in the third quarter and took the lead. Wide receiver Michael Tims finished the drive when he scored on a reverse play that caught Michigan's defense off guard. Washington State led 13-7 and it stayed that way after James Hall blocked Lindell's extra point attempt. Michigan responded on their next drive when Brian Griese threw a 58-yard touchdown pass to Tai Streets. (Bentley Historical Library [BHL], Michigan's Bowl Game History, 1998 Rose Bowl, Page 1)

Craig Baker gave Michigan a 14-13 lead with his second extra point. The third quarter ended with Michigan clinging to their slim one-point lead. (BHL, Michigan's Bowl Game History, 1998 Rose Bowl, Page 1)

Michigan extended their lead early in the fourth quarter after a key defensive stop. Brian Griese led the Wolverines to their final score when he completed his third touchdown pass—23-yards to tight end Jerame Tuman. Kraig Baker's extra point extended Michigan's lead to 21-13. Rian Lindell closed the gap to 21-16 with a 48-yard field goal. Michigan led 21-16 with just over seven minutes to play in the game. (BHL, Michigan's Bowl Game History, 1998 Rose Bowl, Page 1)

Image 13: Brian Griese helped lead Michigan to a perfect record (12-0) in 1997. He was named the Most Valuable Player in the 1998 Rose Bowl. Permission: Bentley Historical Library, University of Michigan.

The Wolverine offense had one more possession and they made it count even though no points were scored. Brian Griese led his team on a sixteen-play drive that devoured almost seven minutes (6 minutes and 56 seconds) of precious playing time. Michigan punted and WSU started their final drive from the seven-yard line with twenty-nine seconds to play. Ryan Leaf almost pulled off a miraculous game winning drive but he ran out of time. Michigan won this epic battle by a final score of 21-16. (BHL, Michigan's Bowl Game History, 1998 Rose Bowl, Page 1) Hail to the Victors and Go Blue!

Season Summary:

The Wolverines were named national champions by the Associated Press and their mission was complete! Now, they were sitting on top of college football's highest mountain, although they had to share some of the space with Nebraska! Yes, Lloyd Carr, the former "interim" coach at Michigan, did something that had not been done at Michigan in almost fifty years.

Coach Carr took the Wolverine football team to the first perfect 12 win and 0 loss season and half of the national championship—one step at a time! Michigan reached the summit of the college football world on January 1, 1998. They enjoyed a spectacular view that Michigan players and coaches had not experienced since 1949 when Bennie Oosterbaan led his Wolverines to a perfect record (9-0-0) and the national championship.

Lloyd Carr's "mountain climbing" metaphor inspired his players and kept them focused on taking one step at a time. The 1997 Wolverine football climbed their way to a very special place in Michigan Football history. They left an incredible legacy for all Michigan football teams that followed them.

The 1997 Michigan football team had a super-talented roster. Three of the best Wolverines earned special honors. Heisman Trophy winner Charles Woodson became a two-time All-American and defensive end Glen Steele and tight end Jerame Tuman were also honored as two of America's best college football players.

Ten Wolverines were named All-Big Ten first team players after Michigan's outstanding season. Of course, Woodson, Steele, and Tuman led the way. Defensive backs Andre Weathers and Marcus Ray also joined the elite group along with quarterback Brian Griese, center Zack Adami, guard Steve Hutchinson, tackle Jon Jansen, and linebacker Sam Sword.

Image 14: There is no doubt that Lloyd Carr's first bowl win was also his most memorable. Michigan's 21-16 win over Washington State clinched a share of the national championship for Michigan. You can't end a season any better than that! Permission: Bentley Historical Library, University of Michigan.

Lloyd Carr's Coaching Milestones:

The third year of the Lloyd Carr Era in Ann Arbor turned out better than any could have ever expected—especially Lloyd Carr. He achieved a career's worth of memories in just one incredible season.

First, he achieved his first, and only, twelve-win season which was also the first perfect 12-0 season in the glorious history of Michigan football.

Second, he also earned half of the national championship from the Associated Press.

Third, Carr earned his first Big Ten Championship with a perfect conference record of eight wins and no losses.

Fourth, Lloyd Carr earned his first victory over another rival with a 21-14 win over Notre Dame on September 27, 1997.

Fifth, Coach Carr posted his twenty-fifth career win with a 24-3 victory over Minnesota on November 1, 1997.

Sixth, he earned his first victory over Wisconsin, the school that did not hire him for their head coaching job in 1989. Yes, I am certain that the 26-16 victory over the Badgers on November 15, 1997 was special.

Seventh, Lloyd Carr also notched his first bowl win on January 1, 1998 with the 21-16 victory over Washington State.

In addition to the wins and championships, Coach Carr also earned a truckload of honors for that special season in 1997. First, he earned Big Ten Coach of the Year.

Second, he was named the Bear Bryant Coach of the Year.

Third, he also accepted the trophy for being the Walter Camp Coach of the Year.

Finally, Lloyd Henry Carr was also inducted into the Detroit Area Catholic League Hall of Fame after the 1997 season. Yes, Coach Carr was a popular and busy man in late early 1997.

CHAPTER 6

How About an Encore?
Season Four - 1998

After two winning seasons in 1995 and 1996, Lloyd Carr's Wolverines won it all in 1997. Okay, they won half of "it all" since Michigan won the Associated Press National Championship Trophy, but not the coaches' trophy from ESPN/USA Today. Anyway, Coach Carr had a different problem in 1998. What would he and his merry band of Wolverines do for an encore? Would they be able to win back-to-back titles like Michigan did in 1947 and 1948? Coach Carr knew that the 1997 team was special. He lost many talented players including Heisman Trophy winner Charles Woodson who left early for the NFL. It appeared that the Wolverines would be coming down from the top of the mountain. The big question was, "How far would they fall?"

Just like Bennie Oosterbaan before him, winning a national title so early in your coaching career can be a blessing and a curse. It is a blessing because you are on top of the world for a brief time, your supporters are legion, and you can't do anything wrong. However, it can be a curse because the national championship becomes the new standard. Annual expectations become unrealistic and almost impossible to fulfill. Like most coaches who get to the top of the mountain, the only way to go is down. It rarely works out any other way.

Team #119 – 1998   Record: 10 wins and 3 losses
Big Ten Champions

The pollsters thought Michigan might land in a good place. The Wolverines were ranked as the fifth-best team in the country at the start of the 1998 season.

September 1998: 2 wins and 2 losses

The co-defending national champions started the season at Notre Dame. The Irish showed no respect for Carr's team and sent the Wolverines back to Ann Arbor with a 36-20 loss. Syracuse came to Ann Arbor in week two and left with a surprising 38-28 win over Michigan. After two games, the Wolverines were sitting on a record of 0 wins and 2 losses.

Image 16: Anthony Thomas scored three touchdowns and Tom Brady and Drew Henson each threw a touchdown pass to lead Michigan to the first victory of the 1998 season. Permission: Bentley Historical Library, University of Michigan.

Image 15: Lloyd Carr talks to tight end Mark Campbell during Michigan's 59-20 win over Eastern Michigan on September 19, 1998. Permission: Bentley Historical Library, the University of Michigan.

Michigan won big in their final non conference game against Eastern Michigan (59-20). Now, the Wolverines could shift their attention to the Big Ten season. Coach Carr's team had a record of 1 win and 2 losses heading into the last week of September. The final game of the month was a home game against Michigan State. Michigan defeated the Spartans (29-17) to even their September record at 2 wins and 2 losses. The best news was that they were undefeated in the Big Ten with a record of 1 win and 0 losses.

October 1998: 4 wins and 0 losses

The Wolverines began the month of October with a hard-earned road win in Iowa (12-9). Michigan pushed their conference record to 3 wins and 0 losses with another hard-fought victory over Northwestern (12-6). Coach Carr's team wasn't blowing anyone out but they were scoring enough points to win some close games. Thankfully, Michigan's stingy defense was only allowing about ten points per game in Big Ten competition. The Wolverine defense stayed on script and the Wolverines posted a 21-10 win over the Indiana Hoosiers. The Maize and Blue footballers finished October with another good win at Minnesota (15-10).

November 1998: 3 wins and 1 loss

Lloyd Carr's Wolverines continued their winning ways in November. The offense woke up and the defense shut down Penn State (27-0) in Ann Arbor. Wisconsin came to town and went back to Madison with a 27-10 loss. This victory clinched at least a share of the Big Ten Championship with just one conference game to play. Of course, that final game was going to be in Columbus against the hungry Buckeyes. Unfortunately, John Cooper finally beat Lloyd Carr and his Wolverines. Yes. the bad news was that Michigan lost at OSU (31-16). The good news was that the Wolverines still earned a share of the 1998 conference championship since their record of 7 wins and 1 loss matched those of Wisconsin and Ohio State.

The Wolverines had one more game on their regular season in 1998 and it was in Hawaii. Michigan ended their regular season with a 48-17 win over the Rainbow Warriors.

Citrus Bowl: January 1, 1999 #15 Michigan 45 #11 Arkansas 31

Michigan entered their final game of the 1998 season as an underdog against #11 Arkansas. However, Jay Feely's 43-yard field goal gave the Wolverines a 3-0 lead after fifteen minutes of football. The Razorbacks took a 7-3 lead early in the second quarter. Carr's team bounced back with two straight touchdowns. Anthony Thomas scored on a 2-yard run and Ian Gold scored on a 46-yard pick-six. Michigan led 17-7 for a few minutes before Arkansas scored on a field goal which cut the Wolverine lead to 17-10. Michigan scored again after a 69-yard drive that ended on a 5-yard run by Anthony Thomas. Jay Feely's third extra point gave Michigan a 24-10 halftime lead. (BHL, Michigan's Bowl Game History, 1999 Citrus Bowl, Page 1)

Arkansas came back to tie the game at 24-24 after three quarters of football. Then, the Razorbacks scored early in the fourth quarter and regained the lead at 31-24. Michigan stormed back with three straight touchdowns.

First, Anthony Thomas scored his third touchdown from 3-yards to tie the game at 31-31. A few minutes later, Tom Brady threw a 21-yard touchdown pass to DiAllo Johnson. Jay Feely made his fifth extra point and Michigan led 38-31. Finally, Michigan defensive back James Whitley ended the last Razorback drive with a 26-yard "pick-six." Feely's sixth extra point ended the scoring. Coach Carr and his Wolverines left Florida with a 45-31 win. (BHL, Michigan's Bowl Game History, 1999 Citrus Bowl, Page 1)

Tom Brady threw for 209-yards and one touchdown. Running back Anthony Thomas ran for 132-yards and scored three touchdowns. He was named the Most Valuable Player of the 1999 Citrus Bowl. Michigan finished their season on a two-game winning streak thanks to their win at Hawaii and their "upset" victory over Arkansas. (BHL, Michigan's Bowl Game History, 1999 Citrus Bowl, Page 1)

Season Summary:

Michigan ended the 1998 season with a record of 10 wins and 3 losses. The Wolverines earned their second straight conference championship and posted double-digit wins for the second straight season. All things considered; it was a very good season for Lloyd Carr's team.

The Wolverines closed the season at #12 in the in the final Associated Press rankings.

Co-Captain Jon Jansen was the only Wolverine to earn All-American honors in 1998.

Tight end Jerame Tuman earned first team All-Big Ten honors for the third straight season and Jansen and guard Steve Hutchinson achieved the honor for the second straight season.

Lloyd Carr's Coaching Milestones:

As expected, there were some more career coaching milestones for Lloyd Carr's fourth season at Michigan. As a matter of fact, there were four. Michigan's first win of the 1998 season was Coach Carr's first win against his former employer—Eastern Michigan. The Wolverines dominated the Eagles that day since they posted a 59-20 victory.

Second, the win over EMU marked the highest point total (59) that a Michigan team ever posted in the Carr Era.

Third, Michigan's 27-0 victory over Penn State on November 7, 1998, was Lloyd Carr's twenty-fifth Big Ten win.

Finally, Coach Carr took his Wolverines to Hawaii for the last game of the regular season on November 28, 1998. It was the only time that Ohio State was not the final game of a regular season during the Lloyd Carr Era at Michigan.

CHAPTER 7

How About a Big Ten Threepeat?
Season Five - 1999

Lloyd Carr was back for season number five in 1999. If Carr's first two seasons fell below expectations, the second two probably exceeded them. Michigan won a national championship and two conference titles in the last two years and nobody in Ann Arbor wanted it to stop! The Wolverines were loaded with talent on both sides of the ball. Yes, expectations would be high again for Coach Carr's football team. After all, he was coaching at Michigan! Once again, the pollsters thought that Michigan would be an excellent football team in 1999 and they started the season off at number seven in the national rankings.

Team #120 – 1999   Record: 10 wins and 2 losses

September 1999: 4 wins and 0 losses

The Wolverines started well in 1999 since Carr's seventh ranked footballers defeated Notre Dame 26-22. They closed out the rest of the non-conference schedule with wins over Rice (37-3) and Syracuse (18-13). Michigan opened the Big Ten season with a hard-fought win at Wisconsin. It is always tough to beat the Badgers in Madison but the Wolverines prevailed 21-16. Carr's Wolverines closed out September with a perfect record of 4 wins and 0 losses for the month and a record of 1 win and 0 losses in conference play. So far, so good.

October 1999: 2 wins and 2 losses

Michigan kicked off the month of October with a 38-12 Homecoming Day victory over Purdue. Carr's Wolverines rose to #3 in the polls. Then, eleventh ranked Michigan State stopped Michigan cold with a 34-31 upset in East Lansing. Things got worse in week seven since Illinois beat the Wolverines in the Big House (35-29). Coach Carr's team got off the mat with a 34-31 win over Indiana. Unfortunately, Michigan's conference championship hopes took a hit with the back-to-back losses to Michigan State and Illinois. Lloyd Carr would have to keep his team focused and hope for a miracle in November.

November 1999: 3 wins and 0 losses

Michigan started November with a 37-3 win over Northwestern in The Big House. The sixteenth ranked Wolverines traveled to Pennsylvania and returned home with a 31-27 victory over Penn State. Coach Carr's team ended the regular season on a positive note with a 24-17 over Ohio State. The good news was that Michigan ended the regular season on a four-game winning streak. The bad news was that they did not win a third straight Big Ten Title. Carr's footballers finished in a tie for second place in the Big Ten with a record of 6 wins and 2 losses.

Orange Bowl: January 1, 2000 #8 Michigan 35 #5 Alabama 34 (OT)

The underdog Wolverines trailed for most of the game against the Crimson Tide. However, they came back every time. Michigan was down 14-0 late in the first half. In the final minute, Tom Brady hit David Terrell with a 27-yard touchdown pass and Hayden Epstein converted the extra point . Alabama led 14-7 at halftime. (BHL, Michigan's Bowl Game History, 2000 Orange Bowl, Page 1)

Early in the second half, Tom Brady and David Terrell connected again for a 57-yard touchdown and Epstein's conversion tied the game at 14-14. Alabama responded with two straight touchdowns to take a 28-14 lead. Carr's Wolverines responded with two straight scores to tie the game. Tom Brady hit David Terrell for the third time for a 20-yard touchdown. A few minutes later, Anthony Thomas scored on a 3-yard run. Hayden Epstein kicked his third and fourth extra points to tie the game at 28-28 after forty-five minutes of football. There was no scoring in the fourth quarter so the game went to overtime. (BHL, Michigan's Bowl Game History, 2000 Orange Bowl, Page 1)

Michigan had the first overtime possession and they made it count. Tight end Shawn Thompson caught a 25-yard scoring pass from Tom Brady. Hayden Epstein made the all-important extra point to give Carr's Wolverines a 35-28 lead. Alabama responded with a touchdown but the extra point kick failed. (BHL, Michigan's Bowl Game history, 2000 Orange Bowl, Page 1) Michigan earned an exciting 35-34 win over Alabama. It was the first overtime game in Michigan football history and it ended well for Coach Carr and his Wolverines!

Season Summary:

Michigan ended the 1999 season with a record of 10 wins and 2 losses. The Wolverines began the season with five straight wins which included two consecutive Big Ten victories. Unfortunately, two straight October losses to Michigan State and Illinois knocked them out of the Big Ten Championship race.

As always, Coach Carr was able to right the ship and get the Wolverines back on track after two tough losses. Michigan finished strong with five straight wins. All things considered, it was another excellent season for Lloyd Carr's and his football team.

The Wolverines closed the season at #5 in the final Associated Press and ESPN/*USA Today* football polls.

Co-Captains Steve Hutchinson (offensive guard) and Rob Renes (defensive tackle) earned first team All-American honors in 1999.

Hutchinson and Renes also earned first team All-Big Ten honors along with receiver David Terrell, tackle Jeff Backus, linebacker Ian Gold, and defensive back Tommy Hendricks.

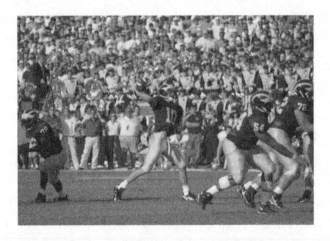

Image 17: Tom Brady's breakout season in 1999 was recognized with his selection as team MVP at the end of the year. Permission: Bentley Historical Library at the University of Michigan.

Unfortunately, Tom Brady did not win any national or conference awards in 1999. However, he was selected as the Most Valuable Player on the 1999 Wolverine football team. Obviously, the people in Ann Arbor knew that Tom Brady was a special football player long before the rest of the football world. Go Blue!

Lloyd Carr's Coaching Milestones:

There were three milestones to highlight about the 1999 season. First, Coach Carr earned his 50th career win the 26-22 victory over Nore Dame on September 4, 1999.

Second, Lloyd Carr, and his Wolverines, won the first overtime game in Michigan football history with their 35-34 victory over Alabama in the Orange Bowl.

Finally, Coach Carr's team achieved something in 1999 that had only been accomplished twice in Michigan football history. The Maize and Blue footballers won ten or more games for the third straight season. Fielding Yost was the first Michigan football coach to achieve that feat when his teams won eleven games in 1901, 1902, and 1903. Bo Schembechler was the second Wolverine coach to achieve double digit wins in three consecutive seasons when his Maize and Blue footballers won ten or more games in 1971, 1972, 1973. Now, Lloyd Carr was a member of that elite group of Michigan football coaches. Very impressive!

CHAPTER 8

Carr Leads Michigan Into the Future
Season Six - 2000

Lloyd Carr was back for his sixth season in 2000. Michigan football was still in good hands with Coach Carr in charge. He was doing things just the way Wolverine Nation liked it. He had already won two Big Ten Championships and one national Championship. Life was good in Ann Arbor. Coach Carr had plenty of excellent players coming back on both sides of the ball. Once again, the pollsters figured that Carr would have another excellent football team in 2000. As it turned out, they were correct.

Team #121 – 2000
Big Ten Champions

Record: 9 wins and 3 losses

September 2000: 4 wins and 1 loss

Sixth ranked Michigan began the 2000 season with a big win over Bowling Green (42-17). Michigan's first victory of the season was also Coach Carr's fiftieth win at Michigan. So far, so good! The Rice Owls suffered a similar fate in game two since they lost to the Wolverines by a score of 38-7. Game three did not go as well for the Maize and Blue. Michigan traveled to California to play UCLA. Unfortunately, Carr's footballers lost to the Bruins (23-20).

Michigan closed out September 2000 and opened the Big Ten season with a 35-31 win at Illinois. Carr's Wolverines made history with their second conference win when they defeated Wisconsin (13-10). Yes, Michigan's fourth win of the season was the 800th victory in the illustrious history of the Wolverine football program. The good news was that Coach Carr's football team ended September 2000 with a record of 4 wins and 1 loss. However, the best news was that Michigan had a perfect Big Ten record of 2 wins and 0 losses.

The Wisconsin game was also the first game that Drew Hensen ever started at Michigan. He led the Wolverine offense to over 375-yards of offense (118-yards rushing and 257-yards passing). Wisconsin's defense kept Michigan out of the end zone for the first three quarters of the game. The Wolverine defense, despite being short four starters, put Michigan in position to win the game. Carr's team had posted two field goals and five turnovers against the Badgers but Michigan still trailed 10-6 in the fourth quarter. With about six minutes remaining in the game, Hensen led the Wolverines to the end zone. He threw a fifteen-yard scoring pass to David Terrell. Jeff Del Verne kicked the extra point that gave Carr's team a 13-10 lead and the points needed for victory #800.

Again, it was a historic win for Coach Carr and the Michigan Wolverine football program. (*Detroit Free Press*, 10/01/2000, Page 12D)

Image 18: Drew Hensen's first start as Michigan's quarterback resulted in Michigan's 800th program victory. Permission: Bentley Historical Library, University of Michigan.

October 2000: 2 wins and 2 losses

Michigan began the month of October with a trip to Lafayette, Indiana. It ended badly since the Wolverines lost to Purdue (32-31). Michigan's record dropped to 4 wins and 2 losses halfway through the season. Carr's footballers tuned-up for their MSU series game with a 58-0 win over Indiana in week seven. It looked like the offense was playing well and the defense was getting healthier. The sixteenth-ranked Wolverines showed the MSU Spartans who was boss with a 14-0 victory in Ann Arbor. October ended on a bad note just like it started—with another upsetting road loss. The Northwestern Wildcats were ranked (#21) and ready for #12 Michigan since they earned a 54-51 shootout victory. That loss put a damper on Michigan's conference championship hopes. Now, the Wolverines would have to win their last two games and get some help. Yes, Carr's football team would need a lot of help!

November 2000: 2 wins and 0 losses

Michigan's unusual schedule resulted in only two games in November 2000. The Wolverines had to make both games count! Carr's footballers kicked off their final month of the season with a 33-11 win over Penn State. Michigan's chances for a championship did not look good since the teams ahead of them kept winning. All the nineteenth ranked Wolverines could do was upset #12 Ohio State and hope for a miracle. The Maize and Blue footballers finished strong with a 38-26 victory in Columbus. As it turned out, Michigan got the help that was needed. The Wolverines ended the conference season with a final record of 6 wins and 2 losses. More importantly, they earned a share of the Big Ten Championship.

Citrus Bowl: January 1, 2001 #17 Michigan 31 #20 Auburn 28

Lloyd Carr was on a bowl "roll" since he and his Wolverines had won three straight post-season games. His Maize and Blue footballers took their second possession of the game to the opening score. Thanks to some trickery, Drew Henson took a "flea flicker" pass and tossed a 31-yard touchdown strike to David Terrell. That exciting play ended a 76-yard drive that took just seventy seconds. Thanks to Hayden Epstein's extra point, Michigan led 7-0 after fifteen minutes of football. (BHL, Michigan's Bowl Game History, 2001 Citrus Bowl, Page 1)

Auburn scored on two straight possessions in the second quarter to take a 14-7 lead over Michigan. The Wolverine defense stiffened for the rest of the quarter and the offense went to work. B.J. Askew scored a 4-yard touchdown after Hensen delivered his second scoring pass. Anthony Thomas ran hard for the entire quarter and was rewarded when his 11-yard touchdown run gave Michigan their second lead of the game. Hayden Epstein's extra point gave Michigan a 21-14 lead at halftime. (BHL, Michigan's Bowl Game History, 2001 Citrus Bowl, Page 1)

Anthony Thomas struck again in the third quarter with a 25-yard scoring run. Epstein made his fourth extra point and the Wolverines led 28-14. The Tigers scored a touchdown late in the quarter to cut Michigan's lead to 28-21. The Wolverines mounted one more drive near the end of the quarter. When the drive stalled, Hayden Epstein kicked a 41-yard field goal to give Michigan a 31-21 lead after forty-five minutes of football. (BHL, Michigan's Bowl Game History, 2001 Citrus Bowl, Page 1)

Auburn scored their final touchdown late in the game to reduce Michigan's lead to 31-28. The Wolverines recovered a Tiger onside kick with just over two minutes to play. Carr's offense controlled the ball until time expired. Michigan hung on for an exciting 31-28 victory in the Citrus Bowl. That triumph gave the Wolverines a final record of 9 wins and 3 losses for the 2000 season. Lloyd Carr's sixth season had some highs and lows but it was another good season.

Yes, winning a share of the conference championship and defeating Ohio State made it another successful season in Ann Arbor.

Season Summary:

Michigan ended the 2000 season with a record of 9 wins and 3 losses. The Wolverines earned their second straight conference championship. All things considered; it was a very good season for Lloyd Carr's team. However, I am sure that Coach Carr thought a lot about losing three games by a total of seven points. His offense scored 404 points and averaged 33.7 points per game. Unfortunately, they failed to score their "average" in two of their losses. The defense, which allowed an average of 19.0 points per game was not ready for Northwestern which is why they lost a 54-51 shootout. Yes, winning nine games is an accomplishment but ten more points could have earned him his second perfect season at 12-0. Oh well, that's the way it goes in coaching. Time to move on!

The Wolverines closed the season at #11 in the in the final Associated Press rankings and #10 in the final USA Today/ESPN poll..

Co-Captain Steve Hutchinson and receiver David Terrell both earned All-American honors in 2000.

Terrell and Hutchinson also earned first team All-Big Ten honors along with Anthony Thomas, Jeff Backus, and Larry Foote.

Lloyd Carr's Coaching Milestones:

Once again, Lloyd Carr and his Wolverines made some magical moments happen in 2000. Carr's 63rd career win against Wisconsin on September 30, 2000, was program victory #800 for Michigan football. Yes, that was a big deal.

Second, Carr's football team defeated Indiana 58-0 on Homecoming Day. It was the highest score and the biggest margin of victory for a homecoming game in the Carr Era.

Third, this game was also the only shutout that Carr's footballers ever posted on Homecoming Day.

Finally, Michigan's exciting victory over Auburn (31-28) made Lloyd Carr the first, and only, Michigan coach to record four straight bowl wins.

CHAPTER 9

Was Coach Carr Feeling Lucky?
Season Seven - 2001

Coach Loyd Carr earned a share of his third Big Ten Championship in six years in 2000. Once again, there were some rough spots in the season. Fortunately, Coach Carr's calm demeanor and steady leadership style helped his players regroup and finish strong. The 2001 season was expected to be another winning season in Ann Arbor. The only question was, "How many games would the Wolverines win this year?" One area of concern for Coach Carr's seventh season was his offense. The 2000 team scored the most points in his six-year tenure (404). However, quality linemen like Steve-Hutchinson, Jeff Backus, and Mo Williams were gone. Finding someone to fill the shoes of running back Anthony Thomas was also a concern. The good news in Ann Arbor was that John Navarre gained a lot of experience in his freshman year. He was back for his second full season as Michigan's quarterback. Of course, there was still plenty of talent on the Michigan Football Roster. Nobody was shedding any tears for Lloyd Carr's football team. In fact, Michigan was ranked number twelve in the country which meant that they could be surprisingly good in 2001.

Team #122 – 2001   Record: 8 wins and 4 losses

September 2001: 3 wins and 1 loss

Michigan began the season with a solid win over Miami of Ohio (31-13). A road trip to Seattle in week two did not go as well. The eleventh ranked Wolverines lost to number fifteen Washington (23-18). The Maize and Blue footballers finished their non-conference schedule with a win over Western Michigan (38-21). Coach Carr's team shifted their attention to the Big Ten season. The Wolverines defeated Illinois 45-20 to end September on a two-game winning streak. Of course, they were unbeaten in conference competition.

October 2001: 3 wins and 0 losses

Michigan began the month of October on a positive note with a 20-0 win at Penn State. The Wolverines extended their victory streak to four games with a 24-10 homecoming victory over Purdue. Carr's team journeyed to Iowa and returned to Ann Arbor with a 32-26 win over the Hawkeyes. Michigan's perfect month (3 wins and 0 losses) lifted them to a tie for the top spot in the Big Ten heading into November.

November 2001: 2 wins and 2 losses

The sixth-ranked Wolverines owned a record of 6 wins and 1 loss when they kicked off against the Spartans in East Lansing on November 3, 2001. Michigan State ended Michigan's five-game winning streak with a controversial 26-24 victory over the Wolverines. The Spartans took advantage of an "extra play" that resulted from a "timing problem." The Wolverines thought that the game was over. Michigan had one more chance to win the game but the defense failed to stop MSU and that was that. Coach Carr's footballers bounced back with two straight victories over Minnesota (31-10) and Wisconsin (20-17).

It was time for another season ending showdown with the hated Buckeyes and a new coach named Jim Tressel. Once again, the Big Ten Championship would be decided in Columbus. Unfortunately, Michigan lost to Ohio State (26-20) in the Big House which is always the worst way to end any regular season. That defeat gave the Wolverines a Big Ten record of 6 wins and 2 losses which earned them a second-place finish.

Citrus Bowl: January 1, 2002 #8 Tennessee 45 #17 Michigan 17

Michigan's second straight Citrus Bowl game did not end as well as the one in 2001. Tennessee's offense racked up a season high 45 points against the Michigan defense. The Volunteers also held the Michigan offense to a season low (17 points). Numbers like that only mean one thing—defeat! This one got out of hand early. It was time to close the book for the 2001 season and get ready for 2002.

Season Summary:

The Wolverines finished the 2001 season with a final record of 8 wins and 4 losses. Coach Lloyd Carr didn't figure Jim Tressel and his Buckeyes out in 2001. I know that Carr was already working on a way to change that in 2002!

The Wolverines slipped a lot in 2001 but they still finished the season at #20 in both the *ESPN/USA Today* Coaches poll and Associated Press rankings.

Linebacker Larry Foote and receiver Marquise Walker both earned first team All-American honors in 2001.

Foote and Walker also earned first team All-Big Ten Honors along with offensive guard Jonathan Goodwin and defensive end Dan Rumishek.

Lloyd Carr's Coaching Milestones:

I looked long and hard to find some memorable milestones to share about Coach Carr. Basically, I failed! The only milestone that I can share is that the 2001 season was season seven of the Lloyd Carr Era. It was not his luckiest season, it was not his best season, and it was not his worst season. However, it was over on January 1, 2002.

CHAPTER 10

Time for Another Championship?
Season Eight - 2002

Speaking of the clock, the Big Ten made a change to their game timing policy for the 2002 season. This was the result of the infamous "Clock Gate" incident at the end of the 2001 Michigan vs. Michigan State game. Now, all conference games would be officially timed by a neutral official on the field. It was a year too late as far as Lloyd Carr was concerned.

The Wolverines began the 2002 season with all the typical questions about who was going to replace some of the stars who graduated. Lloyd Carr lost many key starters. Fortunately, he had some very good players coming back. Quarterback John Navarre was back to run the Michigan offense and the defense was expected to be solid. It looked like Michigan would be ready to compete for another Big Ten Championship along with Ohio State and Iowa.

Team #123 – 2002   Record: 10 wins and 3 losses

August 2002: 1 win and 0 losses

Thirteenth-ranked Michigan began the 2002 season with an "upset" win over eleventh-ranked Washington in Ann Arbor. Coach Carr's Wolverines led 14-13 at halftime but saw themselves trailing late in the fourth quarter (29-28). Kicker Philip Brabbs nailed a 44-yard field goal on the last play of the game to secure a hard-fought victory.

September 2002: 3 wins and 1 loss

Michigan rose to #7 in the country and pounded Western Michigan (35-12) in week two. A road game at Notre Dame did not go well. The 20th ranked Irish sent the Wolverines home with their first loss (25-23). The Maize and Blue footballers slipped to #14 in the rankings, but they did not slip against Utah, at least not totally. Carr's team defeated the Utes (10-7) in a battle of two very good defenses. Michigan was ready for the Big Ten season to begin. The Wolverines ended the month of September with an impressive 45-28 Big Ten road victory against Illinois.

October 2002: 2 wins and 1 loss

The Wolverines began October with a 27-24 win over #15 Penn State. Carr's eleventh ranked footballers pushed their conference record to 3 wins and 0 losses with a 23-2 win over Purdue. Even though Michigan climbed back up to #8 in the country, Iowa was not impressed. The Hawkeyes ruined Homecoming Day in Ann Arbor with a 34-9 victory over the Wolverines. Even though Michigan ended October on a sour note, Coach Carr's team was still in the hunt for a share of the Big Ten Championship. All they had to do was win out in November which is always easier said than done.

November 2002: 3 wins and 1 loss

Michigan started another winning streak with a 49-3 victory over Michigan State. Then the thirteenth ranked Wolverines traveled to Minnesota and came home with a 41-24 victory. The Wolverines remained perfect in November after they defeated Wisconsin 21-14 on Senior Day in Ann Arbor. The final home victory of the 2002 football season was special because it was Coach Lloyd Carr's 75th win at Michigan.

It was time for a very important football game at Ohio State. Yes, Michigan headed into the OSU game with a chance to win a share of the conference championship. The only problem was that Ohio State does not like to share, especially with Michigan. The #2 Buckeyes defeated the #12 Wolverines at the Horseshoe by a score of 14-9. That defeat meant that the Wolverines had to settle for a third-place finish in the Big Ten (6 wins and 2 losses) in 2002.

Outback Bowl: January 1, 2003 #12 Michigan 38 #22 Florida 30

The Wolverines ended the season the same way they started it—with an exciting victory against a ranked opponent. However, this one did not go down to the final play of the game like the season opener against Washington in August.

Michigan was favored to win this encounter against Florida but it wasn't easy. The Wolverines opened the scoring late in the first quarter after a Florida turnover. Chris Perry ran for a 4-yard touchdown. Adam Finley's extra point gave the Maize and Blue a 7-0 lead at the end of the first quarter. (BHL, Michigan's Bowl Game History, 2003 Outback Bowl, Page 1)

The Gators scored two straight touchdowns to start the second quarter but only one extra point to take a 13-7. Carr's Wolverines responded with a long drive that Perry finished with a 1-yard leap into the end zone on fourth down. Finley's second extra point gave Michigan a 14-13 lead late in the quarter. (BHL, Michigan's Bowl Game History, 2003 Outback Bowl, Page 1)

Florida regained a 16-13 lead after a field goal in the last two minutes of the first half. John Navarre led the Maize and Blue "two-minute" offense to the end zone in less than two minutes. He threw an 8-yard scoring pass to Ronald Bellamy and Finley converted his third extra point. Michigan took a 21-16 lead to the locker room at halftime. (BHL, Michigan's Bowl Game History, 2003 Outback Bowl, Page 1)

The Gators scored a touchdown and an extra point on their first possession of the second half to take a 23-21 lead. Coach Carr's Wolverines responded with seven points of their own. Chris Perry's third touchdown (7-yard run) and Epstein's fourth extra point gave Michigan a 28-23 lead. Later in the third quarter, Perry ended another Wolverine drive with a 12-yard run. Hayden Epstein converted his fifth point. The Maize and Blue football team led 35-23 at the end of forty-five minutes of football. (BHL, Michigan's Bowl Game History, 2003 Outback Bowl, Page 1)

Florida scored again with about eight minutes remaining in the game to reduce the Wolverine advantage to 35-30. Late in the game, a Victor Hobson sack forced a Florida punt. Michigan drove the ball deep into Gator territory. When the drive stalled, Adam Finley nailed a 33-yard field goal to increase the Wolverine lead to 38-30. Florida had one more possession that reached the Michigan 37-yard line before Victor Hobson stepped up again. He picked off a Gator pass and that was that! Michigan won a shootout in Tampa—38-30. (BHL, Michigan's Bowl Game History, 2003 Outback Bowl, Page 1)

Quarterback John Navarre passed for a career high 319-yards and one touchdown. Running back Chris Perry rushed for 85-yards and four touchdowns. He was named the Most Valuable Player of the 2003 Outback Bowl. Victor Hobson's big plays late in the game helped Michigan secure an exciting win over Florida. (BHL, Michigan's Bowl Game History, 2003 Outback Bowl, Page 1)

Season Summary:

Michigan's final record in 2002 was 10 wins and 3 losses. A ten-win season is always a worthy achievement. However, a second straight loss to Ohio State left a bad taste in every Wolverine's mouth in 2002. Coach Carr had to find a way to stop Jim Tressel and his Buckeyes in 2003.

The Wolverines closed the 2002 football season at #9 in the *ESPN/USA Today* Coaches poll and #9 in the final Associated Press rankings.

Tight end Bennie Joppru and cornerback Marlin Jackson both earned All-American honors in 2002.

Marlin Jackson also earned first team All-Big Ten honors in 2002 along with versatile offensive lineman Tony Pape (four starts at left tackle and 9 starts at right tackle), offensive guard Dave Baas, linebacker Victor Hobson.

Lloyd Carr's Coaching Milestones:

Lloyd Carr's eighth season had a pair of special moments. First, Coach Carr led his team to victory in Michigan's first regular season overtime game on October 12, 2002. Yes, #15 Penn State gave the Wolverines all they could handle. Fortunately, #13 Michigan prevailed 27-24 in the extra period of football.

Second, on November 16, 2002, Michigan defeated Wisconsin 21-14 in the Big House. It was Coach Carr's 75th career victory as Michigan's Head Football Coach.

CHAPTER 11

Another Championship Campaign
Season Nine – 2003

Lloyd Carr entered the 2003 season with high expectations and a high national ranking (#4) to match. Michigan was loaded with talent. Quarterback John Navarre was back to lead a potentially explosive offense. Chris Perry would be the featured running back and Braylon Edwards was expected to catch a lot of passes. Coach Carr's offense was primed to score more points than team #123 posted in 2002. The defense was an impressive collection of hungry talent. Eight players with starting experience were eager to shut down their opponents and limit their points. The 2002 defense allowed a total of 265-points. The defenders on Team #124 were determined to allow fewer points in 2003 and win more games.

Team #124 – 2003 Big Ten Champions
Record: 10 wins and 3

August 2003: 1 win and 0 losses

Fourth ranked Michigan kicked off the 2003 season with Coach Carr's fourth and final game in the month of August. The Wolverines defeated Central Michigan by a score of 45-7 to get the season off to a winning start.

September 2003: 3 wins and 1 loss

The Wolverines began the month of September with big wins over Houston (50-3) and Notre Dame (38-0). Third-ranked Michigan traveled to Oregon (#22) for their final non-conference game and returned with a 31-27 loss to the Ducks. Michigan won their Big Ten opener over Indiana 31-17.

October 2003: 3 wins and 1 loss

Coach Carr took his ninth ranked Wolverines to Iowa for the first game in October 2003. It did not go well since the #23 Hawkeyes defeated Michigan 30-17. The Wolverines bounced back and went on a small roll for the rest of the month. Michigan traveled to Minnesota and defeated the Gophers (38-35). Then, they ended the month with two straight blowouts—a 56-14 win over Illinois and a 31-3 victory over Purdue.

November 2003: 3 wins and 1 loss

Michigan rose back to #11 in the rankings as they headed to East Lansing for another football battle with #9 Michigan State. The Wolverines "upset" the Spartans and their fans with an exciting 27-20 victory. Michigan was still in the Big Ten Championship race with a conference record of 5 wins and 1 loss. The Wolverines remained in the title hunt with a big win over Northwestern (41-10). It looked like #5 Michigan was as ready as they needed to be for the regular season finale against Ohio State.

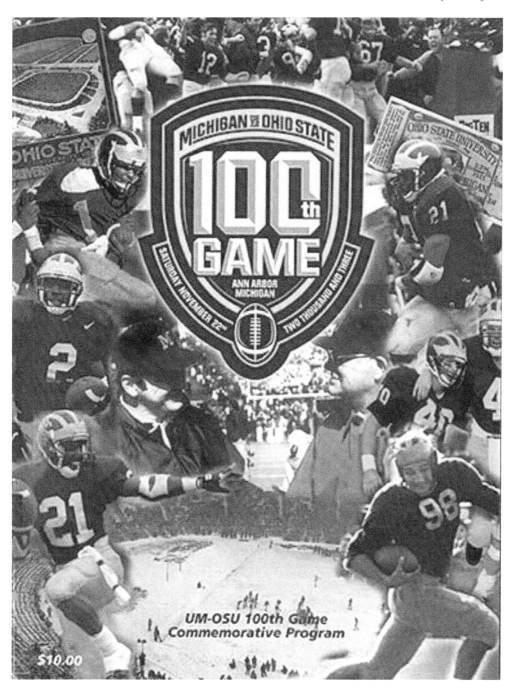

Image 19: Series game #100 between Michigan and Ohio State was played on Saturday, November 22, 2003 in Ann Arbor. Both teams wanted to win the Century Game—for sure! Fortunately, Michigan prevailed 35-21 in the Big House. Permission: Bentley Historical Library, University of Michigan.

As it turned out, Michigan was ready for Jim Tressel and his fourth ranked Buckeyes. The Wolverines defeated Ohio State 35-21 in the 100th game of this storied rivalry. Michigan's decisive victory clinched the Big Ten Championship with a final record of 7 wins and 1 loss. The best news is that they didn't have to share the title with anyone, especially Ohio State!

<u>Rose Bowl</u>: January 1, 2004 #1 Southern California 28 #4 Michigan 14

Michigan's six game winning streak came to a sudden halt in the Rose Bowl. It ended with a disappointing loss to Southern California (28-14). Although both teams were ranked in the top four in the polls, Southern California was clearly the better team. Michigan could not stop the Trojan offense and they didn't score enough points. Of course, that is always a formula for losing a game.

<u>Season Summary</u>:

Coach Lloyd Carr's Wolverines ended the season with a final record of 10 wins and 3 losses. It was another successful season in Ann Arbor but Coach Carr and his staff probably didn't spend a lot of time celebrating. The highest scoring team in the Lloyd Carr Era averaged 35.4 points per game but came up short of that lofty total in all three losses. Carr had to figure out how to score more points, allow fewer, and win more games in 2004. Of course, another Big Ten Championship would also be a goal for Carr's tenth season.

Team #124 closed the season at #6 in the Associated Press poll and #7 in the *ESPN/USA Today* Coaches poll.

Star running back Chris Perry earned All-American honors for his outstanding season in 2003.

Perry earned first team All-Big Ten honors along with quarterback John Navarre, receiver Braylon Edwards, and offensive tackle Tony Pape.

Lloyd Carr's Coaching Milestones:

The 2003 season had a large number of memorable milestones that must be documented. First, the season opening game against Central Michigan was Lloyd Carr's one-hundredth game as Michigan's Head Football Coach. Of course, the 45-7 victory over the Chippewas put a smile on his face. It also sent about 100,000 Michigan fans home in a very good mood. Hail to the Victors!

Second, game one of the 2003 football season was played on August 30, 2003. It was Coach Carr's fourth and last game in August. You may remember that he posted his first career win on August 26, 1995. Lloyd Carr fared well in four August games since he finished with a perfect record of 4 wins and 0 losses during the eighth month of the year.

Third, Michigan traveled to Minneapolis, Minnesota to play in the 100th anniversary game of the famous "Little Brown Jug" game. The Wolverines returned home with a 38-35 win over the Gophers. It was Coach Carr's 50th Big Ten win.

Fourth, the Wolverines trailed by twenty-one points (28-7) heading into the final quarter of this game. The Maize and Blue footballers put the pedal to the metal and scored thirty-one points in the final fifteen minutes to claim the biggest comeback in Michigan football history! It was also the first time that a Wolverine team scored thirty-one points in the fourth quarter.

Fifth, October 18, 2003, was another special day for Lloyd H. Carr since his team defeated Illinois 56-14. It made his homecoming day and sent the alumni home in a good mood. I am sure that Coach Carr always enjoyed a win over Illinois. Remember, Illinois fired Gary Moeller, Lloyd Carr, and a bunch of other coaches in 1979. Yes, any victory over Illinois made Coach Carr smile—especially one with a 42-point victory margin. Go Blue!

Sixth, Michigan's 31-3 win over Purdue was the 350th victory in the glorious history of The big House. Amazing!

Seventh, Lloyd Carr's fifth ten-win season led to his fourth Big Ten Championship.

Finally, Coach Carr's 2003 team was the second one to score over four hundred points during his tenure. In fact, Team #124 scored 460 points which was the highest point total in the Lloyd Carr Era. Michigan scored an average of 35.4 points per game and allowed 16.8 points per game. Those numbers yielded a point differential of 18.6 points per game which was the best in Coach Carr's tenure.

CHAPTER 12

A Decade in the Big Ten
Season Ten – 2004

If season ten of the Lloyd Carr Era turned out like most of his first nine years, it promised to be another successful football season in Ann Arbor. The Wolverines had plenty of excellent players returning for the 2004 season. In fact, Carr had seven men on offense and seven on defense that had all started at least one game in 2003. Coach Carr's biggest challenge was replacing All-American tailback Chris Perry and All-Conference quarterback John Navarre. Yes, Lloyd Carr had to find a work-horse running back and a quarterback to throw the ball to Braylon Edwards and Michigan's other talented receivers. As it turned out, two freshmen emerged in fall practice. Chad Henne earned the right to start at quarterback and Mike Hart lined up at running back when #8 Michigan kicked off the 2004 season. The Wolverines were defending champions in 2004 and they looked like they could win their second straight Big Ten Title.

Team #125 – 2004 *Record: 9 wins and 3 losses*
Big Ten Champions

September 2004: 3 wins and 1 loss

Lloyd Carr's talented team began the season with a big win over Miami of Ohio (43-10). However, game two at Notre Dame was a disappointment since the Wolverines lost (28-20) to the Irish. Michigan finished the non-conference portion of their 2004 schedule with a 24-21 win over San Diego State. The Wolverines looked like a championship contender once conference play began. Carr's footballers defeated Iowa (30-17) to end September, and start the Big Ten season, on a positive note.

October 2004: 5 wins and 0 losses

Michigan journeyed to Bloomington Indiana and returned to Ann Arbor with a 35-14 win over the Hoosiers. Carr's Wolverines defeated Minnesota (27-24) to push their season record to 5 wins and 1 loss. A trip to Champaign, Illinois resulted in a 30-19 win over the Fighting Illini. Purdue hosted Michigan and gave Carr's team a tough battle before falling to the Wolverines by a score of 16-14.

The Maize and Blue football team had a record of 7 wins and 1 loss and a #12 ranking heading into MSU Week. It was time for another battle with Michigan State. The Wolverines defeated the Spartans but it was not easy. It took three overtimes, but Michigan posted a 45-37 victory.

The 2004 series game between the Wolverines and Spartans turned out to be the first overtime game in the history of Michigan Stadium. It was also the first overtime game between Michigan and Michigan State. Of course, it was also the first triple overtime game in Wolverine football history.

Image 20: The 2004 Michigan vs. Michigan State game was the first triple overtime game in Michigan football history. It was also Michigan's first triple overtime victory. Permission: Bentley Historical Library, University of Michigan.

November 2004: 1 win and 1 loss

The ninth-ranked Wolverines had a bye week in the first week of November. They were rested and ready on November 13th and it showed with a big victory (42-20) over Northwestern. Coach Carr's team immediately shifted their attention to the next game at Ohio State.

The seventh ranked Wolverines appeared to have the advantage against the unranked Buckeyes. Unfortunately, Ohio State was ready for Michigan. The Buckeyes sent the Wolverines home to ponder a 37-21 defeat. The loss to Ohio State ruined Michigan's chance for the conference championship. Instead, the Wolverines had to share the title with Iowa since both teams ended the season with identical conference records of 7 wins and 1 loss.

Rose Bowl: January 1, 2005 #6 Texas 38 #13 Michigan 37

The thirteenth ranked Wolverines came within one point of upsetting #6 Texas. As it turned out, Michigan's defense could not stop the high scoring Longhorn offense which is why they lost. For the second straight year, Coach Carr's team ended the season on a bad note with a bowl loss to a higher ranked team.

Season Summary:

The bad news was that Michigan finished the 2004 season on a two-game losing streak and posted a final record of 9 wins and 3 losses. The good news was that Coach Carr and his Wolverines earned a share of another Big Ten Championship. Of course, nobody was happy about the loss to the Buckeyes—especially Lloyd Carr!

The Wolverines ended the 2004 season as the fourteenth ranked team in the final Associated Press poll and at number twelve in the last *ESPN/USA Today* Coaches poll.

Four Wolverines earned All-American honors in 2004. Guard David Baas, receiver Braylon Edwards, cornerback Marlin Jackson, and safety Ernest Shazor were recognized for their outstanding efforts during the season.

In addition to the four Wolverines listed above, running back Mike Hart, tight end Tim Massaquoi, defensive tackle Gabe Watson, offensive tackle Adam Stenavich, and offensive guard Matt Lentz all earned first team All-Big Ten Honors.

Lloyd Carr's Coaching Milestones:

Lloyd Carr's tenth season had some more interesting moments that should be noted. First, Michigan was scheduled to play five games in October for the first time in the Lloyd Carr Era. Guess what, the Wolverines won them all and finished the month with a record of 5 wins and 0 losses!

Second, Michigan defeated Michigan State (45-37) in Ann Arbor to claim the first triple overtime win in program history. The win also kept Carr's record perfect in overtime at 3 wins and 0 losses. It was also the first, and only, triple overtime in "Big House" history—so far.

Third, Coach Carr led his team on the field onto the field on October 9, 2004, to play in front of a very large Homecoming Day crowd. In fact, it was the largest alumni gathering to ever watch a game in the Lloyd Carr Era. Yes, 111,518 people is a very large gathering!

CHAPTER 13

Lloyd Carr's Most Challenging Season
Season Eleven - 2005

The 2005 football season was Michigan's 100th year of Big Ten play. It was also the eleventh season in Coach Lloyd Carr's tenure in Ann Arbor. So far, Lloyd Carr's head coaching career in Ann Arbor was filled with a lot of "ups" and a few "downs." Once again, Michigan, along with Ohio State and Penn State, was among the favorites to compete for the conference championship in 2005. Coach Carr had plenty of excellent players coming back. The pollsters thought that the Wolverines might be pretty good since Michigan landed at #4 in the pre-season rankings. Another ten-win season was not hard to imagine for the fourth-ranked Wolverines.

Michigan's Magnificent March to 1,000 Wins

Team #126 – 2005   **Record: 7 wins and 5 losses**

September 2005: 2 wins and 2 losses

The Maize and Blue footballers began the 2005 season with a solid win over a rising Northern Illinois team (33-17). Things did not work out so well the next week against Notre Dame. The rude guests from South Bend left Ann Arbor with a 17-10 upset victory over Michigan. The Wolverines ended their non-conference season with 55-0 romp over Eastern Michigan. Carr's team had a record of 2 wins and 1 loss heading into Big Ten play. Fourteenth-ranked Michigan traveled to Madison for their first conference game and came home on the short end of a 23-20 score. The Wolverines had a record of 2 wins and 2 losses heading into their next game against Michigan State.

October 2005: 4 wins and 1 loss

Lloyd Carr's unranked Wolverines traveled to East Lansing and upset the eleventh ranked Spartans in overtime (34-31). The next game against Minnesota did not go as well since the unranked Gophers defeated #24 Michigan (23-20) in the Big House. The Wolverines bounced back with a victory over undefeated and eighth ranked Penn State. Chad Henne tossed a last second touchdown pass to Mario Manningham and Michigan defeated PSU by a score of 27-25. A trip to Iowa City went well for Carr's Wolverines. The Maize and Blue footballers had to go to overtime but they beat the Hawkeyes (23-20). Michigan ended the month of October on a three-game winning streak thanks to a 33-17 victory over Northwestern. As it turned out, Coach Carr left Iowa City with his 100th career win as Michigan's Head Football Coach. Michigan ended the month of October on a three-game winning streak thanks to a 33-17 victory at Northwestern.

November 2005: 1 win and 1 loss

After a bye week in the first week of November, the Wolverines extended their winning streak to four games with a 41-14 win over Indiana. It was time for #17 Michigan to host #9 Ohio State. Could Carr's men find a way to beat the Buckeyes?

A season ending loss to Ohio State (25-21) ruined Michigan's outside chance for the conference championship. Instead, the Wolverines finished the regular season with a conference record of 5 wins and 3 losses. The third-place Wolverines were invited to the Alamo Bowl to play Nebraska.

Alamo Bowl: December 28, 2005 Nebraska 32 #20 Michigan 28

The twentieth ranked Wolverines finished the season on a bad note with an upsetting loss to unranked Nebraska. The Huskers were rewarded with a win after scoring more points (32) against Michigan than any team all season. Unfortunately, Michigan only scored twenty-one points. It was a painful way to end a super frustrating season. For the record, the season ending bowl loss to Nebraska was Coach Carr's fourth straight loss in a post-season bowl game.

Season Summary:

The Wolverines posted a final record of 7 wins and 5 losses. It was the worst campaign in Lloyd Carr's eleven-year tenure. To add insult to Michigan's wounded pride, the Wolverines were not ranked in either of the nation's final football polls in 2005. Coach Carr knew that he had to get this turned around in 2006.

Michigan had a winning record in 2005 but it felt like a losing season for everyone in Ann Arbor. There were some interesting "firsts" in Lloyd Carr's eleventh season at the helm but they were not good ones. First, this was the first time that his Wolverines lost three home games in one season. Second, this was the first season in the Lloyd Carr Era where Michigan was not ranked in either major poll at the end of the season. Third, it was the first time that there were no first team All-American players at the end of the season. Finally, this was the first time that Michigan did not win at least eight games in Carr's coaching tenure in Ann Arbor.

The only good news about the 2005 season was that Jason Avant, Matt Lentz, Adam Stenavich, and Gabe Watson all earned first team All-Big Ten honors.

Lloyd Carr's Coaching Milestones:

The 2005 season was Lloyd Carr's eleventh at Michigan. There weren't a lot of memorable milestones to document because of five losses and a third-place finish in the Big Ten.

However, there was one significant event that took place on October 22, 2005. Coach Carr took his Wolverines to Iowa and escaped with a 23-20 win over the Hawkeyes. It was his 100th career win at Michigan. Now, his name was in an elite class of Michigan head coaches who won over one-hundred games. Of course, Bo Schembechler had the most with 194 and Fielding Yost posted 165 win during his tenure. Lloyd Henry Carr Jr. was now the third winningest head coach in the history of the winningest program in college football. That's an impressive accomplishment!

The overtime victory of Iowa was the second one of the season since Michigan also defeated Michigan State on October 1, 2005, by a score of 34-31. It was the first, and only, time that a Wolverine team posted two overtime wins in a season and in the same month.

Another notable fact about Carr's 100th win at Iowa City was that it was an overtime victory. Whew, it was close, but his Wolverines pulled it out at the end. This was Lloyd Carr's fifth and final overtime game. It was also his fifth overtime victory. He is the only coach in Michigan football history to post a perfect record of 5 wins and 0 losses in overtime games.

CHAPTER 14

Coach Carr's Wolverines Bounce Back!
Season Twelve - 2006

Coach Lloyd Carr posted another winning season in 2005, but nobody in Ann Arbor was happy about the final record, especially Lloyd Carr. The good news was that the Wolverines won seven games. The bad news was that they lost five games, including the last two games of the season. Overall, things were looking good for Michigan in 2006. Carr had plenty of experienced players returning on offense, defense, and special teams. The sportswriters thought that Michigan would be very good again in 2006 because they ranked the Wolverines at number fourteen to start the season. If Carr's team could stay healthy, there could be another championship team in year twelve of his coaching tenure in Ann Arbor.

Team #127 – 2006   Record: 11 wins and 2 losses

September 2006: 5 wins and 0 losses

Coach Carr's Wolverines kicked off the 2006 season with a 27-7 victory over Vanderbilt. It was the 850th win in Michigan football history. That victory made Michigan the first team in college football history to achieve that lofty milestone. The Maize and Blue footballers rolled to a 41-17 win over Central Michigan in week two. It was time for Michigan's first road game against Notre Dame. It was a very successful trip since the Wolverines left South Bend with a 47-21 victory. After three games, the Wolverines were undefeated with a perfect record of 3 wins and 0 losses. It was time to focus on the Big Ten Schedule and make a run for a championship.

Michigan opened the Big Ten season with a 27-13 win over Wisconsin in the Big House. Then, the Wolverines journeyed to Minnesota and defeated the Gophers (28-14). The sixth ranked Maize and Blue footballers ended September 2006 with a perfect record of 5 wins and 0 losses. They were also 2-0 in the Big Ten and in position to challenge for the conference championship.

October 2006: 4wins and 0 losses

Michigan opened October by hosting Michigan State. The Wolverines sent the Spartans back to East Lansing to ponder a 31-13 defeat. A difficult road trip to Happy Valley ended well since Michigan returned to Ann Arbor with a 17-10 victory over Penn State. Coach Carr's Wolverines entered the third week of October as the fourth ranked team in the country. Iowa came to town and left with a 20-6 loss to the highly ranked Wolverines. Carr's second ranked team ended October with a 17-3 win over Northwestern and a perfect record of 9 wins and 0 losses.

November 2006: 2 wins and 1 loss

For the first time since 1998, Michigan played a non-conference game in the month of November. For the second time since 2004, the Aztecs gave the Wolverines all they could handle before losing to Michigan (34-26). It was time to focus on the rest of the Big Ten schedule.

Image 21: Coach Carr asked Bo Schembechler to speak to his beloved Wolverines in their final home practice before "The Game" in November 2006. Bo died the next day as #2 Michigan traveled to Columbus to face #1 Ohio State. It was a sad time in Wolverine football history. Permission: Bentley Historical Library, University of Michigan.

Carr took his team to Bloomington, Indiana where his Wolverines defeated the Hoosiers (34-3). It was Michigan's tenth straight victory. The decisive win set up the first #1 vs. #2 matchup in the history of the Michigan vs. Ohio State football rivalry. The build up to game #103 in the historic football series was monumental. Former coach Bo Schembechler spoke to Coach Carr's team after Thursday's practice. Sadly, Coach Schembechler died the next day as the Wolverines traveled to Columbus. The Wolverines were in mourning when they stepped on the field in The Horseshoe.

The Maize and Blue footballers battled valiantly in their quest to "Win One for Bo" but it wasn't meant to be. Michigan came up short since Ohio State claimed a 42-39 victory. The Wolverines tied for second place in the Big Ten with a record of 7 wins and 1 loss and earned a spot in the Rose Bowl.

Rose Bowl: January 1, 2007 #8 Southern California 32 #3 Michigan 18

The Wolverines were slight favorites to defeat USC in the Rose Bowl. The game was tied 3-3 at halftime. Unfortunately, the Trojans took charge of the game with sixteen unanswered points in the third quarter. Southern California won the second half and cruised to a 32-18 victory over the Wolverines.

Season Summary:

Michigan's best season since 1997 ended on a sad note (the death of Bo Schembechler) and two bad notes (Ohio State loss and Rose Bowl loss). The Wolverines finished with a final record of 11 wins and 2 losses. Coach Carr and his staff made everyone forget about 2005 but many Michigan fans still hoped for more wins in 2006. Of course, that is a coach's lot in life unless he wins them all!

The Wolverines closed the season at #6 in the final Associated Press poll and #9 in the *ESPN/USA Today* Coaches poll.

Three Michigan stalwarts earned All-American honors in 2006. Cornerback Leon Hall, defensive lineman LaMarr Woodley, and offensive tackle Jake Long were recognized for their outstanding efforts during the season.

Hall, Woodley, and Long also earned first team All-Big Ten Honors along with defensive tackle Alan Branch, linebacker David Harris, offensive guard Adam Kraus, running back Mike Hart, wide receiver Mario Manningham, and kicker Garret Rivas.

Lloyd Carr's Coaching Milestones:

Lloyd Carr's twelfth season was great for the first eleven games since his Wolverines started with eleven consecutive victories. Unfortunately, the last two games against Ohio State and Southern California did not go as well. Carr's team came within nineteen points of a perfect season but it was not meant to be in 2006. Still there were some milestones that must be mentioned.

First, Michigan made more football history on September 2, 2006, when Vanderbilt came to Ann Arbor. The Wolverines defeated the Commodores 27-7. Coach Carr and his players posted the 850th win in Michigan football history. Once again, they achieved something that no other team in college football had ever accomplished! Hail to the Victors!

Second, September 2005 was the first month that saw five games on a Michigan football schedule in the Lloyd Carr Era. The Wolverines blazed through the month and posted a perfect record of 5 wins and 0 losses. Carr's Wolverines outscored their opponents by a margin of 170 points to 72 points in September. Michigan was on a roll as the calendar page turned to October 2006.

Third, Lloyd Carr finished his career with a winning record against Notre Dame. Unfortunately, he had a winless road record of 0 wins and 3 losses against the Irish when he took his Wolverines to South Bend, Indiana. Yes, Coach Carr was overdue for a win in Notre Dame Stadium. On September 16, 2006, the Wolverines delivered for Coach Carr. Eleventh ranked Michigan thumped the second ranked Golden Domers 47-21. I am sure that Lloyd Carr was smiling after his first win in South Bend. Go Blue!

Finally, the unranked Wisconsin Badgers came to Ann Arbor on September 23, 2006, to play the sixth ranked Michigan Wolverines. Coach Carr's Maize and Blue footballers played a solid game and defeated Wisconsin 27-13. It was the last win that Lloyd Carr posted against the team that did not hire him for the head coaching job in 1989. As it turned out, Coach Carr finished with a final record of 7 wins and 2 losses against Wisconsin. He won five Big Ten Championships and one national championship during his tenure at Michigan. Barry Alvarez, who was hired in 1989, did pretty well in Madison. However, he only won two conference championships and no national championships during his career in Madison, Wisconsin. I know that Lloyd Carr always enjoyed a victory over Wisconsin a little more than most teams. Just saying!

CHAPTER 15

Coach Carr's Final Season
Season Thirteen - 2007

Head Coach Lloyd Carr was back for his thirteenth season in 2007. So far, his coaching career at Michigan was a series of winning seasons (12 straight), many Big Ten Championships (five), and a national championship (1997). Yes, talented players occupied just about every key position in Carr's lineup. In fact, Michigan returned eight players on offense with starting experience including All-American tackle Jake Long, All-Big Ten players Mike Hart and Mario Manningham. He also had a healthy Chad Henne at quarterback who was ready to lead Michigan to a Big Ten Championship. The defense was anchored by seven returning veterans. Coach Carr would have to find a placekicker but he had some strong candidates who were eager to prove their kicking prowess. The pollsters thought that the Wolverines would be pretty good since they entered the season as the fifth ranked team in the country. Once again, the Wolverines were expected to compete with the Buckeyes, Penn State, and Iowa for the conference title. Yes, it looked like it would be another winning season for Coach Carr and his Michigan Wolverines.

Team #128 – 2007   *Record: 9 wins and 4 losses*

September 2007: 3 wins and 2 losses

Michigan's first game in 2007 turned out worse than anyone could have predicted. Oh boy, what a shocker! Appalachian State University brought their "Spread Offense" to the Big House and left with the biggest upset in the history of Michigan Stadium! Michigan lost to the Mountaineers 34-32. Wow, nobody saw this coming, especially Lloyd Carr. Michigan dropped completely out of the rankings after their very upsetting loss in game one.

It was the first time that a ranked team ever lost to a Division I FCS team. Week two was even worse as a rising Oregon team showed no mercy. The Ducks went home with a thirty-two-point win (39-7) over the stunned Wolverines. This was one of the worst home defeats in Michigan football history. The Wolverines were sitting at zero wins and two losses in the Big House and had lost two straight to start a season for the first time since 1998. After just two games, the natives were getting restless.

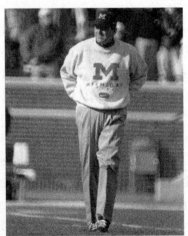

Image 22: Lloyd Carr's team bounced back from their first two losses in 2007 and defeated Notre Dame and Penn State. The win over PSU gave Coach Carr a final record of 9 wins and 2 losses over the Big Ten's newest team. Permission: Bentley Historical Library, University of Michigan.

Once again, Lloyd Carr's steady leadership allowed his team to pick up the pieces and move forward. After the Oregon defeat, Coach Carr did what he did best. He helped his team get up off the mat and get back in the win column in week three.

I asked Coach Carr how he was able to get his team refocused after those two devastating losses. Here is a summary of what he said:

I told my team after the Oregon loss that if we were going to lose two games this season, those two would be the ones to lose. Now, we could focus on winning our next game (Notre Dame) and the Big Ten Championship. I am not going to quit and I know that you're not going to quit. We are going to practice better and play better starting tomorrow. We still have a lot to play for. It's time to move forward.

Yes, Lloyd Carr always seemed to be at his best when his team was not. He was almost uncanny in the way he brought out the best in his players in the most difficult times. Apparently, his positive message hit his team right in the heart.

In week three, Carr's Wolverines blasted Notre Dame (38-0) to get back on the winning side of the ledger. Tenth ranked Penn State came to Ann Arbor for Michigan's Big Ten opener and left with a 14-9 loss.

Michigan ended the month of September with their first road game of the season against Northwestern. It ended well since the Wolverines defeated the Wildcats by a score of 28-16.

The media kept reminding everyone that Michigan began the season with two straight losses. Fortunately, Lloyd Carr and his Wolverines had moved on—big time! Just like 1997, they took it one play and one game at a time. The results were impressive.

October 2007: 4 wins and 0 losses

Coach Carr's team opened their October schedule with a non-conference victory over Eastern Michigan (32-22). Purdue was the next team to play the improving Wolverines. Michigan defeated the Boilermakers handily (48-21). Michigan climbed back into the national rankings at #24. The Wolverine footballers journeyed to Champaign, Illinoi and defeated the Fighting Illini by a score of 27-17. Carr's team posted their seventh straight win with a 34-10 victory over Minnesota. After a terrible start in September, Michigan was perfect (4 wins and 0 losses) in October and in the hunt for another Big Ten Championship.

November 2007: 1 win and 2 losses

Coach Carr took his Wolverines to East Lansing on November 3rd to face off against rookie coach Mark Dantonio and his Spartans. The Spartans led for most of the game but could not finish the job. The Wolverines defeated "Little Brother" 28-24 and left town with the Paul Bunyan Trophy.

Michigan now owned a record of 8 wins and 2 losses. Coach Carr's football team was back in the rankings at number thirteen. The only thing separating Michigan from another season ending battle with Ohio State was unranked Wisconsin. The #13 Wolverines traveled to Madison and returned home to ponder a Badger beatdown since Michigan lost by a score of 37-21. Ouch! Coach Carr and his team knew what they had to do. The eight-game winning streak was over and the chances for another Big Ten Title took a big hit.

Now, it was time to defend their home turf against the hated Buckeyes. Once again, Big Ten bragging rights were on the line again in this historic rivalry. Michigan headed into the OSU game with a chance to win a share of the conference championship. The only problem was that Ohio State does not like to share, especially with the Wolverines. The Buckeyes kept the Wolverines out of the end zone and earned a 14-3 win over Michigan.

Lloyd Carr's team settled for another second-place finish in the Big Ten with a final record of 6 wins and 2 losses. Coach Carr told his team the next day that he would retire after Michigan's bowl game. Carr made it "official" the next day when he announced his plan to hang up his whistle after the bowl game in January 2008. The good news for the unranked Wolverines was that they would play in the Capital One Bowl in Orlando, Florida on January 1, 2008. The bad news was that they would play against the ninth ranked Florida Gators. Florida was the early favorite to win this game since it was in their home state. The Wolverines would have to play one of their best games of the season to send Lloyd Carr out on a winning note.

Capitol One Bowl: January 1, 2008 Michigan 41 #9 Florida 35

Unranked Michigan was the underdog when they took the field to play #9 Florida in the 2008 Capital One Bowl in Orlando, Florida. The Gators had a high-flying offense led by Heisman Trophy winner Tim Tebow and a speedy receiver named Percy Harvin. Coach Carr and his Wolverines definitely had their hands full on News Years Day.

The good news was that the game started with a score of 0-0 when Florida kicked off to Michigan. Chad Henne led the Michigan offense on a 93-yard drive that took twelve plays. Henne ended it when he threw a 21-yard touchdown pass to Mario Manningham. K.C. Lopata's extra point gave Carr's Wolverines a 7-0 lead. Later in the quarter, Florida evened the game on a 10-yard scoring pass From Tebow to Harvin. The game was tied 7-7 at the end of the first quarter. (BHL, Michigan's Bowl Game History, 2008 Capital One Bowl, Page 2)

Florida took a 14-7 lead in the second quarter on a Tim Tebow touchdown pass to Andre Caldwell. Michigan came back to tie the score with a twelve-play drive that took almost five minutes. Mike Hart ended the 56-yard scoring march with a 3-yard touchdown run. It was his 40th career rushing touchdown as a Wolverine. K.C. Lopata's extra point tied the game 14-14. Michigan's defense stepped up to stop Florida's next scoring drive when Terrance Taylor blocked a Gator field goal attempt. Michigan scored with eight seconds to play in the first half on a 1-yard pass from Henne to Adrian Arrington. Lopata's third extra point gave Carr's team a 21-14 lead at halftime. (BHL, Michigan's Bowl Game History, 2008 Capital One Bowl, Page 2)

Michigan surprised Florida on the opening kickoff of the second half. The Wolverines called a "pooch-kick" that was covered on the Gator 37-yard line by special teams' captain Anton Campbell. Seven plays later, Mike Hart slammed across the goal line for his second score of the game. K.C. Lopata's fourth conversion increased Michigan's lead to 28-14. Florida's high-powered offense wasn't hitting on all eight cylinders in this game—thanks to Michigan's defense. (BHL, Michigan's Bowl Game History, 2008 Capital One Bowl, Page 2)

Unfortunately, the Gators began to click in the third quarter. Tim Tebow and Percy Harvin went to work and the Gators drove 56-yards in ten plays. Tebow finished the drive with a 1-yard touchdown dive. After the extra point, Michigan's lead was cut to 28-21.

Chad Henne led the Maize and Blue offense all the way to the Florida 1-yard line before Mike Hart fumbled. The Gators covered the ball in the Michigan end zone for a touchback. Tim Tebow took his offense eighty-yards in eight plays. Tebow connected with Andre Caldwell for another touchdown pass and the game was tied 28-28 after forty-five minutes of nail-biting football. (BHL, Michigan's Bowl Game History, 2008 Capital One Bowl, Page 3)

Michigan broke the 28-28 deadlock in the final quarter when K.C. Lopata kicked a 37-yard field goal. Carr's team led 31-28 with just over twelve minutes to play in the game. The good news was that the Wolverine defense stiffened on Florida's next possession and Carr's offense got the ball again. The bad news was that a Chad Henne pass was tipped and intercepted by the Gator defense. (BHL, Michigan's Bowl Game History, 2008 Capital One Bowl, Page 3)

Five plays later, Harvin scored on a 10-yard reverse. Florida regained the lead with just over five minutes to play—35-31. Michigan took the ensuing kickoff and moved the ball rapidly (four plays) into the Gator end zone. Adrian Arrington ended the 67-yard drive when he caught an 18-yard touchdown pass from Henne. Lopata kicked his fifth extra point and Michigan regained a 38-35 lead with just over three minutes to play in the game. The Wolverine bent but didn't break since they stopped Florida on a fourth down play at the Gator 24-yard line. Carr's offense could not get into the end zone but Lopata came through again when he kicked a 41-yard field goal to end the scoring. Michigan led 41-35 and that's how the game ended. (BHL, Michigan's Bowl Game History, 2008 Capital One Bowl, Page 4)

What a game! The Maize and Blue football team rose to the occasion and sent Coach Carr out on a winning note. Chad Henne was the best quarterback on the field in this game, not Heisman Trophy winner Tim Tebow. Henne completed twenty-five passes for 373-yards and three touchdowns. Mike Hart ran for 129-yards and two touchdowns. K.C. Lopata converted five extra points in five attempts and was perfect with two field goals in tries. Michigan's defense limited Tebow to seventeen completions and 153-yards in the air. He also scored a touchdown but it was not enough to overcome the Wolverines.

Lloyd Henry Carr Jr. was carried off the field on the shoulders of his beloved players and into the Michigan football history books.

Season Summary:

Coach Carr's final season ended with a record of 9 wins and 4 losses. Lloyd ended his Michigan coaching career with a final record of 122 wins and 40 losses. His winning percentage was just over seventy-five percent (.753) for all games and just under seventy-eight percent (.779) in Big Ten Conference competition. He led Michigan to the national championship in 1997 and won, or shared, five conference championships. It was an outstanding run for the former "interim" head coach at Michigan.

The Wolverines closed the 2007 season at #19 in the *ESPN/USA Today* Coaches poll and #18 in the final Associated Press rankings.

Jake long earned All-American honors for the second straight season.

Long also earned first team All-Big Ten Honors along with running back Mike Hart, receiver Mario Manningham, and guard Adam Kraus.

Lloyd Carr's Coaching Milestones:

Guess what? Lloyd Carr's thirteenth and final season had a number of coaching milestones to discuss.

First, Coach Carr led his Wolverines onto the field for the 150th time on September 1, 2007. Unfortunately, it was not his most memorable day since Appalachian State upset #5 ranked Michigan.

Second, September 29, 2007, was the day that Coach Carr won his 75th Big Ten game at Michigan. Yes, the 28-16 win over Northwestern put him in a special place among Wolverine coaches.

Third, Lloyd Carr's Wolverines defeated Purdue on October 13, 2007. It was Carr's final homecoming victory. He did a pretty good job of keeping the alumni happy since he posted a final record of 11 wins and 2 losses on that special day in Wolverine football lore.

Fourth, Coach Carr earned his final victory over Michigan State in his last game in East Lansing on November 3, 2007. Michigan's come-from-behind 28-24 triumph was also Carr's final Big Ten win. It was also the 100th game of the Mitten State rivalry. Coach Carr is the only man in Michigan football history to lead the Wolverines to victory in the 100th game against two rivals (Ohio State and Michigan State).

Fifth, Lloyd Henry Carr Jr. posted his final career victory on January 1, 2008, in the Capital One Bowl. The Wolverines sent him out on a winning note with a 41-35 triumph over Florida. It was Coach Carr's 122nd win which put him in third place on the all-time win list behind Bo Schembechler and Fielding Yost.

Finally, January 1, 2008, was also the day that Coach Carr closed his coaching career at Michigan. His thirteen-year tenue was the third longest in Wolverine football history behind Yost (25 years) and Schembechler (21 years). After forty-years as a high school and college coach, it was time to hang up the whistle. Lloyd Carr's Wolverines carried him off the field one last time as he held his head high.

Thank You Coach Carr and Go Blue—forever!

CHAPTER 16

A Closer Look: Coach Carr vs. The Nation

Most of the first fifteen chapters of this book focused on Lloyd Carr's early football career and his thirteen seasons as the University of Michigan's Head Football Coach. Now, it is time to take a closer look at his accomplishments in a variety of areas. This chapter will examine how Lloyd Carr compared to some of the best programs in the country. Yes, his teams were pretty good. This chapter will tell you why his numbers were good enough to get him into the College Football Hall of Fame. Let's learn exactly how good Michigan was during the Lloyd Carr Era.

Overall Records From 1995 to 2007:

Thanks to Lloyd Carr, the Michigan football program continued to be one of the best in college football from 1995 to 2007. Here is a summary of my research into the teams that stood out in the years that Coach Carr roamed the sidelines in Ann Arbor. The numbers displayed on the chart below include bowl games.

Rank	School	Wins-Losses-Ties	Win %
1	Ohio State	130-33	.797
2	Florida	127-38	.770
3	Virginia Tech	126-38	.768
4	Tennessee	125-39	.762
5	Texas	125-39-1	.760
6	Florida State	124-40	.756
7	**Michigan**	**122-40**	**.753**
8	Nebraska	122-43	.739
9	Georgia	118-44	.728
10	Miami (Florida)	116-42	.734
11	Boise State	116-44	.725

This table contains some good news for Lloyd Carr and the Michigan football program. Of course, it also contains some bad news since Ohio State was the winningest team in the country from 1995 to 2007. Yes, the Buckeyes were very good during the years shown above. A few more victories over OSU would have bumped Michigan into the top five teams on this chart. For the record, the Wolverines averaged 9.38 wins per season during this period. Only Ohio State averaged ten wins per year from 1995 to 2007. Every other team on the list achieved from 9.77 to 8.92 wins per season for thirteen years.

The Wolverines were solid during the Carr Era and the numbers confirm that fact. It is interesting to note that Michigan and Nebraska achieved the same number of wins during this period (122) but the Huskers had three more losses (43 to 40). The teams who shared the national championship in 1997 were as close as they could be. Now they are conference rivals!

Offense and Defense 1995 to 2007:

Now, it's time to take a closer look at Coach Carr's offense and defense from 1995 to 2007. The Wolverines scored an average of almost twenty-nine points (28.7) per game during the Carr Era. Four of his teams averaged over thirty points per game including a high of over thirty-five points (35.4) per game in 2003. In addition, eight of Carr's teams averaged over twenty-six points per game. The 1996 team averaged just over twenty-three points (23.1) per game, which was the lowest total of his career.

Year	Games	Won	Lost	Tied	Scored/Avg.	Allowed/Avg.	+/- Difference
1995	13	9	4	0	338/26.0	223/17.2	+8.8
1996	12	8	4	0	277/23.1	184/15.3	+7.8
1997	12	12	0	0	322/26.8	144/12.0	+14.8
1998	13	10	3	0	359/27.6	235/18.1	+9.5
1999	12	10	2	0	361/30.1	247/20.6	+9.5
2000	12	9	3	0	404/33.7	229/19.1	+14.6
2001	12	8	4	0	320/26.7	237/19.8	+6.9
2002	13	10	3	0	361/27.8	265/20.4	+7.4
2003	13	10	3	0	460/35.4	219/16.9	+18.5
2004	12	9	3	0	370/30.8	279/23.3	+7.5
2005	12	7	5	0	345/28.8	244/20.3	+8.5
2006	13	11	2	0	380/29.2	207/15.9	+13.3
2007	13	9	4	0	354/27.2	278/21.4	+5.8
Totals	162	122	40	0	4651/28.7	2991/18.5	+10.2

Coach Carr's defenders allowed an average of over eighteen points (18.5) per game. The best defensive numbers were posted by the 1997 team.

The Wolverines only allowed one hundred and forty-four points for that special season which averaged out to twelve points per game. Five of Carr's teams allowed more than twenty points per game (1999, 2002, 2004, 2005 and 2007) with the high average being over twenty-three points (23.3) per game in 2004.

Coach Carr's point differentials were positive for every season. His best point differential was in 2003 when his Wolverines were about eighteen (18.5) points better than their opponents for the entire season. His second-best point differential was in 1997. The Wolverines were solid on both sides of the ball and produced a point differential of over fourteen points (+14.8) which was good enough for a perfect season and a piece of the national championship.

In the final analysis, Lloyd Carr's teams were solid on offense and defense. His Wolverines did not dominate the way Bo's teams did in the 1970s. Of course, that statement could be made for just about every coach in America from 1995 to 2007. Coach Carr finished with a positive point differential of over ten points (+10.2) per game. Four of Lloyd Carr's teams (1997, 2000, 2003 and 2006) posted double digit point differentials with the highest being over eighteen points (+18.5) per game in 2003. The 1997 team averaged about twenty-seven (26.8) points per game. Team #118 only allowed twelve points per game which is why they were about fourteen points better than their opponents in that magical season.

Overall, Coach Lloyd Carr had thirteen straight winning seasons during his tenure. His 2003 and 2006 teams were also very strong on both sides of the ball. Coach Carr's teams were consistent and competitive. Ten of his thirteen teams won nine or more games including eight teams that won ten games. Of course, his national championship team, that finished with twelve wins and no losses (12-0-0), was his best and one of the best in Michigan Football History! Coach Lloyd Carr's winning rate was just over seventy-five percent (.753) for the one hundred sixty-two games that he served as Michigan's Head Football Coach.

In the final analysis, nobody shed any tears for Michigan in May 1995 when Gary Moeller resigned. However, many Big Ten coaches shed some tears and lost their jobs while Lloyd Carr was on the Michigan sidelines. Carr continued the work of Bo and Mo and coached himself into the College Football Hall of Fame. Not bad for a guy who started out as an "interim" fill in. Eventually he became one of the most successful, and most respected, coaches in Michigan football history.

Number One and Top Ten Confrontations

During Lloyd Carr's tenure, the Wolverines had twenty-six opportunities to play teams that were ranked in the top ten. This included two games against a number one ranked team. (USC 2004 in the Rose Bowl and Ohio State in 2006). Unfortunately, they lost both of these confrontations. Overall, Carr posted an excellent record of seventeen wins and nine losses against top ten teams for a winning rate of almost sixty-seven percent (.667).

Games	Won	Lost	Tied.	Scored/Avg.	Allowed/Avg.	+/-
27	18	9	0	354/29.5	330/27.5	+2.0

Regular Season Non-Conference Matchups

Michigan fared pretty well in non-conference games from 1995 to 2007. Coach Lloyd Carr led his team in forty-five non-conference games during his thirteen-year tenure at Michigan. Overall, he won thirty-five of those games and only lost ten for a winning rate of seventy-seven percent. Coach Carr won thirty non-conference games in the Big House and only lost four times for an amazing winning rate of eighty-eight percent. His Wolverines were not as good on the road and finished with five wins and six losses in Carr's thirteen seasons.

Home Games	Won-Lost	Win %
34	30-4	.882
Away Games	**Won-Lost**	**Win %**
11	5-6	.454
Total Games	**Won-Lost**	**Win %**
45	35-10	.777

Michigan's Magnificent March to 1,000 Wins

Here is a listing of all the non-conference opponents that the Wolverines faced during the regular season from 1995 to 2007. As you can see from the numbers below, Carr's teams did very well when they played out of the Big Ten. Michigan has always had a consistent scheduling philosophy for non-conference games which is to play good teams from all over the country. The Wolverines like to stay home as much as possible in non-conference games, but if it takes a home and home series to play better teams then so be it.

Non-Conference Opponent Summary 1995-2007

Teams	Games	W-L	Teams	Games	W-L
Appalachian State	1	0-1	Notre Dame	9	5-4
Ball State	1	1-0	Oregon	2	0-2
Baylor	1	1-0	Rice	2	2-0
Boston College	2	2-0	San Diego State	1	1-0
Bowling Green	1	1-0	Syracuse	2	1-1
Central Michigan	2	2-0	UCLA	2	1-1
Colorado	2	2-0	Utah	1	1-0
Eastern Michigan	2	2-0	Vanderbilt	1	1-0
Hawaii	1	1-0	Virginia	1	1-0
Houston	1	1-0	Washington	2	1-1
Memphis	1	1-0	Western Michigan	2	3-0
Miami of Ohio	3	3-0			
Northern Illinois	1	1-0	**Column Total**	26	17-9
Column Total	19	18-1	**Final Total**	45	35-10

National Rankings

Lloyd Carr's teams were very consistent in the polls at the end of each football season. In fact, only the 2005 season did not finish with a top twenty-five ranking. His teams were ranked in the top twenty teams, or higher for his first ten seasons. Unfortunately, the 2005 team finished with 7 wins and 5 losses, which wasn't good enough for a final ranking. His 2006 team bounced back to finish at number six in the AP poll and number nine in the CNN/USA Today Coaches poll. His last team finished at number eighteen in the AP poll and number nineteen in the final CNN/USA Today Coaches poll.

Overall, Coach Carr's Wolverines earned two final rankings in the top five (1997 and 1999) and three more rankings from number six to ten (2002, 2003 and 2006). Coach Carr and his Wolverines earned a special place in Michigan Football History with their amazing performance in 1997. It still irks many Michigan fans that they finished first in the AP poll and second to Nebraska in the CNN/USA Today Coaches poll. However, as my dear mother used to say, "Half a loaf is better than none!"

Image 23: Lloyd Carr's teams were ranked in the top twenty teams in the country at the end of every season in the Carr Era except 2005. Permission: Bentley Historical Library, University of Michigan.

Bowl Games

Lloyd Carr took his Wolverines to a bowl game in every season that he was the Head Coach of the Michigan Football program. After losing his first two bowl games, he went on a roll from 1998 thru 2001 and became the first, and only, Michigan Football Coach to win four straight bowl games. Unfortunately, Coach Carr also had a streak of four straight bowl losses (three Rose and one Alamo), which is second to Bo's streak of seven straight bowl losses. Overall, Lloyd Henry Carr Jr. finished with six bowl victories and seven bowl losses in thirteen games.

A Closer Look at the "Margins"

One interesting area I enjoyed researching was the margins—the margin of victory and the margin of defeat in the Lloyd Carr Era. This particular graphic gives us a look at how Coach Carr's teams fared in the close games, the blowouts, and everything in between. Here is a closer look at how Michigan did in their 162 games from 1995 to 2007.

Victory Margin	# Wins	Loss Margin	# Losses
1 to 5 points	31	1 to 5 points	21
6 to 10 points	18	6 to 10 points	8
11 to 15 points	17	11 to 15 points	5
16 to 20 points	17	16 to 20 points	3
21 to 25 points	11	21 to 25 points	1
26 or more points	28	26 or more points	2
Totals	**122**	**Totals**	**40**

The numbers shown above tell us that the Carr's Wolverines were consistent and competitive against the "Margins." From 1995 to 2007. The Wolverines footballers played in a total of fifty-two "close" games that were decided by five points or less. They won thirty-one of those games and lost twenty-one. They had positive margins (more wins in each category than losses) in every category on this chart. The Wolverines were dominant at times winning twenty-eight games by more than twenty-six points. They only had two "blowout" losses. The "margins" chart clearly shows that the Wolverines won a lot of games in the Lloyd Carr Era.

All-American Players

Almost every major college football program has a large number of good football players. What makes the difference is the number of very good players and the great players that occupy a spot on a team's roster. This has been the case ever since Michigan started playing football in 1879 and it remained that way from 1995 to 2007. Let's take a closer look at the quality of players who played for Coach Lloyd Carr and Michigan during this era.

Coach Lloyd Carr continued Michigan's tradition of attracting great players to play college football in Ann Arbor. In his thirteen seasons, Coach Carr had twenty-three players who earned a total of twenty-seven All-American selections. Eleven players on offense earned All-American honors and so did twelve defenders. Carr had a pair of players on offense and defense who were two-time All-American players. You can't be any more consistent than that!

Yes, four of his players—Charles Woodson, Marlin Jackson, Steve Hutchinson, and Jake long—were two-time selections.

Coach Carr had at least one All-American player in every season except 2005. He had two seasons (1996 & 2004) that produced four All-American selections. Carr had three All-American selections in 1997 and 2006. Lloyd Carr had a reputation for being a fair man so his "All-American" numbers were about as fair as you can get! Here is a list of the Michigan football players who earned All-American honors from 1995-2007:

Coach Carr's Defensive All-Americans (11/13)

Defensive Back – Charles Woodson (1996-97), Marlin Jackson (2002 & 2004), Ernest Shazor (2004), and Leon Hall (2006)

Defensive Tackle – Jason Horn (1995), William Carr (1996), Glen Steele (1997), Rob Renes (1999)

Defensive End – LaMarr Woodley (2006)

Linebacker- Jarrett Irons (1996), Larry Foote (2001)

Coach Carr's Offensive All-Americans (12/14)

Center – Rod Payne (1996), David Baas (2004)

End – Jerame Tuman (1997), David Terrell (2000), Marquise Walker (2001), Bennie Jopru (2002), Braylon Edwards (2004)

Halfback – Chris Perry (2003)

Offensive Guard – Steve Hutchinson (1999 and 2000)

Offensive Tackle – John Runyan (1995), Jon Jansen (1998), Jake Long (2006-2007)

Michigan's strong tradition of All-American players continued from 1995 through 2007 thanks to Coach Lloyd Carr and his staff.

Summary

The Lloyd Carr Era was very good for Michigan Football, especially the first ten years. He won at a high rate (.753) and took Michigan to the top of the college football mountain in 1997. He also won five Big Ten Championships in thirteen years. Overall, Coach Carr's teams performed at a consistently high level. The Wolverines were still among the best teams in the nation for thirteen years. Michigan Football was in a good place when Lloyd Carr retired in January 2008.

CHAPTER 17

A Closer Look:
Coach Carr vs The Big Ten

When you examine the Big Ten Conference from 1995 to 2007, the first thing that strikes you is that the math does not add up. The Big Ten conference expanded to eleven teams when Penn State joined the conference in 1995. For "branding" issues the conference with eleven teams would continue to be called the Big Ten. (Try explaining that to a nine-year old grandchild.) Overall, it was quite a fiasco because of the way it was handled. The university presidents completed the entire process on their own. All conference athletic directors were left out of the picture until it was a "done deal." Bo was amazed and miffed that Michigan President Duderstadt didn't want his input about such an important issue. Schembechler figured that if Duderstadt didn't need to consult with Bo about such an important issue, it was time to move on. So, Schembechler left Michigan to the become the President of the Detroit Tigers.

I used seven criteria to measure Michigan's success against the rest of the Big Ten Conference from 1995 to 2007. First, I looked at the overall record, all games against all opponents, during this twenty-one-year period. Second, I examined the total number of conference wins that Coach Carr posted during this time period and compared them to the rest of the Big Ten teams for this era. Third, I detailed the number of conference home wins for Coach Carr from 1995 to 2007. Next, I examined the number of conference road victories that he earned in this era. Fifth, I reported the number of conference championships the Wolverines were able to win during this time period and how their accomplishments compared to the rest of the teams in the league. Sixth, I summarized the record that Coach Carr posted against all conference teams during his thirteen years as head coach. Finally, I examined the number of All-Conference players that played at Michigan during Carr's thirteen years. A closer look at these factors yields a clear picture of where Coach Lloyd Carr and his Wolverines stood in the Big Ten Conference from 1995 to 2007.

Overall Conference Wins – 1995 to 2007

The chart on the next page is a summary of my research into the victories earned by all Big Ten Conference teams from 1995 to 2007. These wins include all bowl wins earned during this era. (Note: This data was gathered from the Bentley Historical Library and the USA Today College Football Encyclopedia).

Yes, the Michigan football was in a good place if you consider that they were ahead of nine other teams in total wins during this era. The bad news for the Wolverine coaches, players, and fans was that they were behind the Buckeyes again. Everyone at Michigan worked hard to stay ahead of Ohio State from 1969 to 2000. Unfortunately, the Buckeyes worked even harder from 2000 to 2007 to nudge ahead of the Wolverines in overall performance.

Team	Games	Won	Lost	Tied	Win %
Ohio State	163	130	33	0	.798
Michigan	**162**	**122**	**40**	**0**	**.753**
Wisconsin	163	110	52	1	.675
Penn State	159	103	56	0	.648
Purdue	159	90	68	1	.569
Iowa	157	88	69	0	.560
Michigan State	156	80	75	1	.516
Northwestern	155	74	81	0	.477
Minnesota	155	72	83	0	.465
Illinois	150	55	94	1	.370
Indiana	148	47	101	0	.318
Totals	**1,727**	**971**	**752**	**4**	**.563**

Another fact to note about the conference at this time is that it was still not completely over the previous era of the Big Two and the Little Eight. Michigan and Ohio State won at a much higher rate than everyone else in the conference. Of course, the Wolverines represented the conference in an exemplary manner in 1997 when the Wolverines shared the national championship with a future Big Ten partner—Nebraska. They became the first conference team to win a national championship since 1968. The Buckeyes followed Michigan's lead and won it all in 2002. Nobody else in the conference was at that level which meant that the conference, as a whole, slipped during this era.

The Big Ten was still an outstanding conference, but definitely not the strongest conference in college football. Great teams from the Southeast Conference, the Big Twelve Conference, and the Atlantic Coast Conference were now winning plenty of national championships.

Conference Wins from 1995 to 2007

The chart below shows the total number of conference wins that each Big Ten team achieved from 1995 to 2007.

Team	Games	Won	Lost	Tied	Win %
Michigan	104	81	23	0	**.779**
Ohio State	104	80	24	0	.769
Wisconsin	104	62	41	1	.601
Penn State	104	59	45	0	.567
Purdue	104	55	48	1	.533
Iowa	104	54	50	0	.519
Northwestern	104	47	57	0	.452
Michigan State	104	45	58	1	.433
Minnesota	104	34	70	0	.326
Illinois	104	31	72	1	.303
Indiana	104	23	81	0	.221
Totals	1,352	571	569	4	.423

Despite numerous surges by many conference teams, things looked a lot like they did in the Big Ten from 1968 to 1994. The Wolverines were on top and the Buckeyes were right behind them. Michigan was one win better than Ohio State. Nobody else was close.

Coach Carr's Conference Record – Michigan Stadium

The wins at Michigan Stadium had been steady in the Schembechler and Moeller Eras. It was Lloyd Carr's job to keep that trend going from 1995 to 2007. Let's take a closer look at how well Lloyd Carr did in his efforts to win as many conference home games as possible and keep the Wolverine Faithful satisfied.

Year*	Games	Won	Lost	Tied	Scored/Avg.	Allowed/Avg.	+/-
1995	4	3	1	0	101/25.2	59/14.7	+10.5
1996	4	3	1	0	109/27.2	86/21.5	+5.7
1997	4	4	0	0	95/23.7	47/11.7	+12.0
1998	4	4	0	0	104/26.0	37/9.2	+16.8
1999	4	3	1	0	128/32.0	67/16.7	+15.3
2000	4	4	0	0	118/29.5	21/5.2	+24.3
2001	4	3	1	0	120/30.0	66/16.5	+13.5
2002	4	3	1	0	106/26.5	75/18.7	+7.8
2003	4	4	0	0	153/38.2	55/13.7	+24.5
2004	4	4	0	0	144/36.0	98/24.5	+11.5
2005	4	2	2	0	109/27.2	87/21.7	+5.5
2006	4	4	0	0	95/23.7	35/8.7	+15.0
2007	4	3	1	0	99/24.7	54/13.5	+11.2
Totals	52	44	8	0	1481/28.4	786/15.1	+13.3

*Bold Year = Big Ten Championship Season

In the end, Lloyd Carr's work against Big Ten teams at Michigan Stadium was exceptional. His conference winning percentage of just under eight-five percent (.846) at the Big House was second only to Bo in Michigan Stadium history.

Lloyd Carr's teams were very difficult to beat at the corner of Stadium Boulevard and Main Street which was just fine with Wolverine Nation. He had six undefeated seasons in conference play and six more one-loss campaigns. Coach Carr's "worst" home season was in 2005 when his Wolverines broke even in conference play at two wins and two losses.

Lloyd Carr did not lose two conference home games until his eleventh season at Michigan. This is one of those overlooked statistics that a lot of people don't know about, but it is an impressive accomplishment. Carr always went about his business in a quiet, unassuming way. However, the results he posted were impressive, especially in the Big House. Overall, Michigan was a consistent conference winner at home in Big Ten games during the Lloyd Carr Era. The Wolverines competed frequently for the Big Ten Championship and won five of them.

Coach Carr's Conference Record – Away Games

Winning Big Ten road games is always a difficult task. Lloyd Carr served on the staffs of both Bo and Mo. He knew about the preparation that was required for Big Ten road games. He knew the dangers of places like East Lansing, Happy Valley, West Lafayette, Columbus, and other venues that could put a loss on the ledger quicker than a fumbled punt return at your own ten-yard line. Coach Carr knew the formula for Big Ten success—win a large number of your home games and steal as many as you can on the road. Let's see how well Lloyd Carr did at following the two best conference road show coaches in Michigan football history.

Lloyd Carr's "road show" did not begin like Gary Moeller's. Instead, it was more like Bo's conference road adventures. Coach Carr won his first Big Ten road game at Indiana before losing to the Spartans in East Lansing, just like Bo did.

Coach Carr's footballers were not as dominant in their Big Ten road games as Schembechler and Moeller, except for the 1997 season. That special season was Carr's only undefeated conference road campaign. However, Lloyd Carr never posted a losing record for Big Ten road games.

Year*	Games	Won	Lost	Tied	Scored/Avg.	Allowed/Avg.	+/-
1995	4	2	2	0	114/28.5	86/21.5	+7.0
1996	4	2	2	0	76/19.0	45/11.3	+7.7
1997	4	4	0	0	120/30.0	31/7.8	+22.0
1998	4	3	1	0	55/13.8	56/14.0	-.20
1999	4	3	1	0	117/29.3	108/27.0	+2.3
2000	4	2	2	0	155/38.8	143/35.8	+3.0
2001	4	3	1	0	96/24.0	69/17.3	+6.7
2002	4	3	1	0	118/29.5	87/21.8	+7.7
2003	4	3	1	0	133/33.3	95/23.8	+9.5
2004	4	3	1	0	102/25.5	84/21.0	+4.5
2005	4	3	1	0	110/27.5	91/22.8	+4.7
2006	4	3	1	0	118/29.5	69/17.3	+12.2
2007	4	3	1	0	104/26.0	94/23.5	+2.5
Totals	52	37	15	0	1418/27.3	1058/20.3	+7.0

*Bold Year = Big Ten Championship Season

The Wolverines scored thirty points per game and allowed about eight points per game in 1997. It is difficult to lose games with a positive point difference of twenty-two points per game. That level of performance on both sides of the ball is why Michigan was perfect in conference play and every other game as well! Michigan scored an average of twenty-seven points per game in thirteen years and allowed an average of just over twenty points per game (20.3).

Eight of Carr's teams allowed over twenty points a game with the worst being the 2000 team. That group allowed over thirty-five points (35.8) per game. Coach Carr's Wolverines had positive point differentials in every conference road season except 1998, but still managed to win three out of four games—most of them close. Michigan posted a positive point differential of seven points per game during the Carr Era, which meant they were in every conference road game and usually made things difficult for their Big Ten hosts.

Coach Carr was a good student and he learned his Big Ten road lessons well. No, he wasn't as good as Bo or Mo, but he put together some really good road shows during his tenure. Lloyd Carr's first two years in conference road games finished even—four wins and four losses. After that, Michigan won thirty-three games and lost eleven for a winning rate of seventy-five percent which was closer to the conference road records of Bo and Mo. In the final analysis, Lloyd Carr was really tough to beat in conference home games, but he was no slouch on the road either. Overall, Coach Carr had a winning rate of just over seventy-one percent (.711) percent in fifty-two Big Ten road games.

Coach Carr's Final Conference Record 1995-2007

Lloyd Carr final Big Ten winning percentage was almost seventy-eight percent (.779). Yes, it was not as good as Bo's, but nobody in the history of the Big Ten has ever matched Coach Schembechler's numbers! Coach Carr's body of work in conference play was outstanding. He had a winning conference record in every season that he coached and the worst that he did was finish in fifth place in 1996. His teams were very consistent on both sides of the ball and were almost always in contention for the conference title.

In thirteen years of coaching, Coach Carr's Wolverines averaged almost twenty-eight points per game and allowed just over seventeen in one hundred and four conference games. His teams scored an average of thirty points per game in four different seasons and averaged over twenty points in every year he coached in the conference except for 1998. Carr's highest scoring teams (2003 and 2004) both averaged over thirty points per game. His 1998 team was the lowest scoring team of his tenure with point production of just under twenty points (19.9) per game.

Year*	Place	Games	W-L-T	Scored/Avg.	Allowed/Avg.	+/-
1995	Tie 3rd	8	5-3	215/28.5	145/18.1	+8.8
1996	Tie 5th	8	5-3	185/23.1	131/16.4	+6.7
1997	1st	8	8-0	215/26.9	78/9.8	+17.1
1998	Tie 1st	8	7-1	159/19.9	93/11.6	+8.3
1999	Tie 2nd	8	6-2	245/30.6	175/21.9	+8.7
2000	Tie 1st	8	6-2	273/34.1	164/20.5	+13.6
2001	2nd	8	6-2	216/27.0	135/16.9	+10.1
2002	2nd	8	6-2	224/28.0	162/20.3	+7.7
2003	1st	8	7-1	286/35.8	150/18.7	+18.8
2004	Tie 1st	8	7-1	246/30.8	168/21.0	+9.8
2005	Tie 5th	8	5-3	220/27.5	178/22.3	+5.2
2006	Tie 2nd	8	7-1	213/26.6	104/13.0	+13.6
2007	Tie 2nd	8	6-2	203/25.4	148/18.5	+6.9
Totals	--------	104	81-23	2900/27.9	1831/17.6	+10.3

Coach Carr's spectacular defense of 1997 yielded an average of less than ten points (9.8) per Big Ten game which allowed the Wolverines to go undefeated in the conference that year. This was the only team to average less than ten points per contest. Five of his teams allowed an average of over twenty points per game (1999, 2000, 2002, 2004 and 2005). Six of his defenses were able to keep the number of points allowed per game in the teens which helped Coach Carr build a consistent winner in Big Ten competition.

Coach Carr's plus/minus numbers were not spectacular but they were solid. He had a positive point differential in every season and found ways to win even when the numbers were in the single digits. Lloyd Carr's numbers dipped slightly at the end because of his inability to beat the Buckeyes as regularly as he had in his early years.

Conference Championships

As I mentioned in the beginning of the chapter, "familiar" is the word that describes the state of the Big Ten Conference from 1995 to 2007. The Buckeyes set the standard with six championships and Michigan was right behind with five. The conference was competitive for most of this era. However, Ohio State and Michigan were still the dominant teams. Here is a breakdown of how the conference championships were distributed from 1995 to 2007:

School	Titles	Years (T = Tied for Championships)
Ohio State	6	1996(T), 1998(T), 2002(T), 2005 (T) , 2006, 2007
Michigan	**5**	**1997, 1998(T), 2000(T), 2003, 2004(T)**
Wisconsin	2	1998 (T), 1999,
Iowa	2	2002 (T), 2004 (T)
Northwestern	3	1995, 1996 (T), 2000 (T),
Illinois	1	2001
Penn State*	1	2005 (T) (Vacated)
Purdue	1	2000 (T)

Conference Era Summary

Overall, Lloyd Car and his Wolverines played in one hundred and four conference games from 1995 to 2007. They posted a final record of 81 wins and 23 losses. Michigan's conference winning rate for this period was over seventy-seven percent (.779). Coach Carr's teams claimed five conference championships during this era but did not win any after the 2004 season. The bottom line was pretty simple—the Wolverines were still a top-level program for most of this era. Let's take a closer look at Coach Carr's overall performance in the Big Ten from 1995 to 2007.

Carr vs. the Big Ten 1995 to 2007

Team	Won - Lost
Illinois	8-1
Indiana	10-0
Iowa	6-2
Michigan State	10-3
Minnesota	10-1
Northwestern	8-3
Ohio State	6-7
Penn State	9-2
Purdue	7-2
Wisconsin	7-2
Totals	**81-23**

Lloyd Carr continued the winning ways for the Maize and Blue during his tenure. He had a decided advantage against every conference team except Ohio State (6 wins and 7 losses). He was perfect against Indiana and only lost once to Illinois and Minnesota. Iowa, Penn State, Purdue, and Wisconsin beat him twice, but he won twenty-nine of thirty-seven games against these teams for a winning rate of over seventy-eight percent. He lost three games to Michigan State and Northwestern but posted eighteen wins in twenty-four games for a winning rate of seventy-five percent. Lloyd Carr's body of work in the Big Ten Conference was exemplary. His teams added five more league titles, giving the Wolverine's forty-two overall when he retired.

Conference Finish Summary

The numbers below document Coach Carr's conference finishes from 1995 to 2007. The numbers show that Michigan was at or in the top three teams for every season but one (2005).

Place/Result	1995-2007
First:	5 Times 1997, 1998(T), 2000(T), 2003, 2004(T)
Second:	5 Times: 1999(T), 2001, 2002, 2006(T), 2007(T)
Third	2 Times – 1995(T), 2005(T)
Fourth	None
Fifth	1 Time – 1996(T)

All-Conference Players

As expected, Michigan continued to recruit outstanding players to wear the Winged Helmet from 1990 to 2010. Coach Moeller inherited some quality players from Bo and Lloyd started with some from Mo. Overall, the quantity and quality of Wolverine Football players during this era compared favorably with the high standards that Bo had established during his tenure.

Lloyd Carr picked up where Bo and Mo left off and developed fifty-four players who earned a total of seventy-six all-conference selections from 1995 to 2007. He coached Steve Hutchinson, the second player in program history to earn all-conference honors for four straight years (1997-2000). Carr also produced two more players who earned conference honors for three straight years—Charles Woodson (1995-1997) and Jerame Tuman (1996-1998). Coach Carr also worked with fifteen Wolverines who were two-time selectees for Big Ten honors.

In alphabetical order, they were David Baas (2002 & 2004), Jeff Backus (1999-2000), Braylon Edwards (2003-2004), Larry Foote (2000-2001), Jarrett Irons (1995-1996), Marlin Jackson (2002 & 2004), Jon Jansen (1997-1998), Adam Kraus (2006-2007), Matt Lentz (2004-2005), Jake Long (2006-2007), Mario Manningham (2006-2007), Tony Pape (2002-2003), Adam Stenavich (2004-2005), David Terrell (1999-2000), and Gabe Watson (2004-2005).

When it was all said and done, fifty-one Wolverines earned a total of seventy-six first team all-conference selections from 1995 to 2007. A lot of very good players became great players and continued Michigan's superb tradition of outstanding conference play. Their efforts helped to produce one national championship and five conference championships during this period.

Summary

Interim Coach Lloyd Carr picked up the pieces after Gary Moeller's abrupt resignation in May 1995. Carr established his own winning program that delivered a national championship and a Big Ten Title in year three. Carr's teams continued to compete at a high level in conference play until his retirement in 2007. Lloyd Carr added a total of five Big Ten Championships to the Michigan trophy case which brought the Wolverines to a conference best of forty-two titles. Those numbers definitely helped him earn a well-deserved spot in the College Football Hall of Fame.

CHAPTER 18

A Closer Look: Coach Carr's vs. Notre Dame

Times change, but not everything changes, especially in Ann Arbor. The "Big Three" were the same priorities in 1995 as they were in 1948. Yes, the three really big things that a Michigan football coach must accomplish were still pretty simple, just not easy to do. First, he must field teams that can consistently compete at the national level. Second, he must consistently challenge for the conference championship. Finally, he must do well against Michigan's rivals. Of course, there are a myriad of other things that the leader of the winningest college football program in history must achieve, but it starts with items one, two and three. No, this is not rocket science, it's just the way it is at the University of Michigan.

Lloyd Carr knew about the expectations for a Michigan football coach—all of them. He knew that his long-term success hinged on the ability to beat as many teams as possible, especially the teams that mattered a little more.

A Brief History of Michigan's Rivals

Technically, the University of Notre Dame is Michigan's oldest rival since they played their first game against the Wolverines in 1887. The on again-off again series is not played every season. However, what it lacks in "quantity" is more than compensated for by the "quality" of the games between these nationally respected football programs. Historically, this non-conference battle is played early in the season. It is basically an early season "bowl" game that usually serves as a "barometer" for how the rest of the season might go. National bragging rights" are always on the line when the Wolverines and the Fighting Irish meet on the football field.

Michigan and Minnesota played their first game in 1892. The Gophers actually won the first two series games before the Wolverines posted four straight wins between 1895 and 1902. Over the years, the almost annual battle with Minnesota matters a little more because it is a Big Ten game. It also matters more because both teams play for a trophy called "The Little Brown Jug." The Wolverine enjoyed a large advantage in the series when Lloyd Carr took over in 1995. Of course, nobody at Michigan wants to be on a team that loses possession of the Little Brown Jug. Coach Carr knew it was his job to keep Michigan way ahead of Minnesota and build a permanent home for the "jug" in Ann Arbor.

The Michigan-Ohio State rivalry officially kicked off in 1897. It was not much of a rivalry in the early years since the Wolverines went undefeated in the first thirteen games. Ohio State made big gains in the series during the Woody Hayes Era. The rivalry really started to gain national attention when Bo Schembechler arrived in 1969 to challenge Woody's grip on Michigan and the rest of the Big Ten. The Michigan vs. Ohio State game was a really big deal by 1995. The annual winner would probably be the conference champion so the stakes continued to be very high for the annual showdown.

Michigan and Michigan State began their football battles in 1898. The Wolverines started strong against the Spartans and continued to enjoy a large advantage until the Fifties and Sixties thanks to Biggie Munn and Duffy Daugherty.

Things ramped up considerably when Michigan State gained admission to the Big Ten Conference in the early Fifties. The Wolverines and Spartans were now in-state rivals and conference rivals who battled for bragging rights, Big Ten Championships, and a prize named the Paul Bunyan Trophy since 1953. Yes, this game is a big game in the State of Michigan because Michigan and Michigan State just don't like each other. Yes, it is always one of the most intense games that is played in any college football season.

The next four chapters will take a closer look at how Coach Carr and his Wolverines did against the rivals that matter just a little more. (Minnesota and Notre Dame). Of course, others matter a lot more (Michigan State and Ohio State). I will report on each rival in order of their origin date, not the number of games played. It is time to find out how Lloyd Carr did against the "Big Four" rivals during his tenure.

Yes, Lloyd Carr wanted to win every time he led his team onto the field. But, he had a clear understanding of the expectations associated with four special teams: Notre Dame, Minnesota, Ohio State, and Michigan State. All of these contests would fall into the "big" game category on Michigan's schedule. Coach Carr knew that he would be judged a little more harshly for losses against any of the "Big Four" teams. Of course, that's what makes Michigan football so special and Lloyd Carr would not have it any other way.

Michigan vs Notre Dame: The Carr Era 1995-2007

The Michigan-Notre Dame rivalry was technically alive and well when Lloyd Carr took over the program in 1995. However, the teams were on a two-year hiatus for 1995 and 1996. The rivals were not scheduled to meet on the field again until 1997.

Lloyd Carr's first game against Notre Dame was his third game of what turned out to be one of the greatest seasons in Michigan football history.

Carr's unheralded Wolverines were starting to turn some heads after two impressive wins in September 1997. Michigan had moved rapidly up the rankings to number six when the unranked Irish arrived in Ann Arbor. It was a true Michigan vs. Notre Dame contest as the Fighting Irish gave the Wolverines a tough battle before losing by seven points (21-14).

Of course, this game gave the Wolverines a lot of confidence going into the Big Ten season. They went on to run the table and win a share of the national championship for the first time in fifty years.

Game number two, in 1998, did not go as well as Bob Davie's team (ranked number twenty-two) humbled the fifth ranked Wolverines by sixteen points (36-20) in South Bend. This game set up a pattern for the series which saw the home team win every game of the series except one game at each venue. Michigan won four of five games in Ann Arbor and Notre Dame won three of four games in South Bend.

Michigan was ranked in eight of the nine games and was the higher ranked team in seven of the games played during the Carr Era. Michigan was ranked as high as number three (2005), but no lower than eleventh in the eight games that were played between 1997 and 2006. Neither team was ranked when they met in 2007. The Irish were ranked in six of the nine games played coming in at number two in 2006 before suffering a twenty-six-point loss (47-21) to the Wolverines in South Bend. (Lloyd Carr's only win in South Bend was a beauty!) The Irish were ranked between fifteen and twenty-two when they were ranked but did not have a ranking when they played in 1997, 2004 and 2007. Of course, the rankings didn't matter much in this one as every game in the series continued to be a sellout at both stadiums.

Coach Carr won four of the five games played in Michigan Stadium. Lloyd won both games that he played at home against Bob Davie and absolutely blew out Ty Willingham and the Irish by thirty-eight points (38-0) in 2003—the most lopsided victory in series history. He lost his first game to Charlie Weis in 2005 which turned out to be the only Notre Dame game that he lost at home. Lloyd Carr came back in 2007 with a vengeance. His Wolverines humbled the Irish, again, with another thirty-eight-point blowout win (38-0).

Lloyd Carr's teams averaged over twenty-six points (26.6) points per game in Ann Arbor and allowed an average of just over ten points (10.6) per game for a positive point differential of sixteen points per game. Life was good for Lloyd Carr against Notre Dame in the Big House!

Coach Carr vs Notre Dame Head-To-Head 1997-2007

Games	W-L-T	Scored/Avg.	Allowed/Avg.	+/- Difference
Home	4-1-0	133/26.6	53/10.6	+16.0
Road	1-3-0	110/27.5	110/27.5	Even
Totals	**5-4-0**	**243/27.0**	**163/18.1**	**+8.9**

Things didn't go so well for Coach Carr in South Bend, Indiana since he lost three of four games at Notre Dame Stadium. He lost his only game to Bob Davie at South Bend and lost both contests against Ty Willingham's teams at Notre Dame. Lloyd Carr's only win at Notre Dame was the blowout victory (47-21) over Charlie Weis and his team in 2006. Carr's teams were amazingly consistent in their efforts at Notre Dame Stadium. His Wolverines scored one hundred and ten points and allowed exactly one hundred and ten points in four games. This worked out to an average of just over twenty-seven (27.5) points on both sides of the ball at Notre Dame Stadium. That's about as close as it gets in football.

Overall, Coach Carr's teams won five games and lost four games against Notre Dame. He finished with a record of two wins and one loss against Bob Davie. Ty Willingham posted a record of two wins and one loss against Lloyd Carr. Coach Carr was probably sad to see Charlie Weis go since he finished at two wins and one loss along with two of the biggest victory margins in the series. Michigan averaged exactly twenty-seven points per game against Notre Dame in the Carr Era and allowed about eighteen points (18.1) points per game. This worked out to a positive point differential of almost nine points per game (+8.9) which is why Lloyd held the advantage in this highly competitive series when he retired in 2007.

Lloyd Carr did something that Bo could not accomplish from 1969 to 1989. He had a winning record against Notre Dame from 1997 to 2007. Here is what the numbers looked like for Coach Carr vs. Notre Dame:

Games	W-L-T	Scored/Avg.	Allowed/Avg.	+/-
9	5-4-0	243/27.0	163/18.1	+8.9

The numbers shown above paint a favorable picture for Carr's Wolverines in the rivalry from 1997 to 2007. The point differentials that Lloyd Carr's teams posted were impressive. His positive point differential of almost nine points per game was unusual in the history of the series. Michigan was better during this era, but the series was close and so were most of the games.

Michigan vs. Notre Dame Series Summary

Michigan and Notre Dame played a total of nine games during the Lloyd Carr Era. The Wolverines improved their series advantage by winning five of those nine contests.

The chart below shows what the Michigan vs. Notre Dame football series looked like before Lloyd Carr became the head coach. It also shows what he did during his tenure. Finally, the bottom line shows what the rivalry looked like when Coach Carr hung up his whistle in 2007. It is an interesting chart.

Time Period	Won-Lost-Tied	Win %	Michigan Advantage
1887-1994	15-10-1	.596	+5 wins
1995-2007	5-4-0	.556	+1 win
1887-2007	20-14-1	.586	+6 wins

At the end of the 2007 season, Michigan retained a solid advantage in the series that began way back in 1887. The Michigan vs. Notre Dame series is long in history but very short on actual games. The teams only played twenty-six games between 1887 and 1994.

Michigan had a five-win advantage at the start of the Lloyd Carr Era. Coach Carr held his own against the Irish and achieved a winning record in the nine games he coached against Michigan's "first rival." Thanks to Lloyd Carr, the Wolverines still had the advantage over the Fighting Irish at the end of the 2007 season.

Michigan vs. Notre Dame Program Comparisons 1995-2007

Lloyd Carr increased Michigan's advantage against the Irish during his tenure at Michigan. The Wolverines continued to have the most wins in college football history and they bested the Irish in all the important key numbers displayed on the chart below. At the end of the 2007 season, Michigan claimed 869 total wins while Notre Dame totaled 824 program victories. The numbers displayed below show that Michigan was better than Notre Dame from 1995 to 2007—period!

Statistical Area	Michigan	Notre Dame
Total Wins	122	95
Total Losses	40	61
Winning Percentage	.753	.608
Winning Seasons	13	10
Losing Seasons	0	3
Even Seasons	0	0
National Championships	1	0
Top Ten Poll Rankings	6	1
Heisman Trophy Winners	1	0
All-American Selections*	12	1

*Consensus All-Americans

CHAPTER 19

A Closer Look: Coach Carr vs. Minnesota

It should come as no surprise that the Michigan vs. Minnesota rivalry was as one sided in the Lloyd Carr Era as it ever was. His ten victories in eleven games meant that the Little Brown Jug didn't leave Ann Arbor very often from 1995 to 2007. Lloyd Carr knew where the jug belonged and he did an outstanding job of keeping it in Ann Arbor. It is time to take a closer look at how the Wolverines fared against the Golden Gophers during Lloyd Carr's tenure.

Michigan vs. Minnesota: The Carr Era 1995-2007

I am ninety-nine percent certain that Lloyd Carr knew about Bo's record against the Gophers (19 wins, 2 losses, and 0 ties). I also guarantee that he knew that Mo was perfect against Minnesota (5 wins, 0 losses, and 0 ties). Coach Carr was not about to be the one who lost the jug to the Gophers so he went out and won his first eight games against Minnesota. Unfortunately, Glenn Mason ambushed him in Ann Arbor in 2005. Lloyd Carr won the last two games to finish at ten wins and one loss in this "almost" annual rivalry.

Image 24: The Little Brown Jug is one of the most famous trophies in college football. Michigan enjoyed a large advantage in the series and Lloyd Carr kept it that way. Permission: Bentley Historical Library, University of Michigan.

Yes, Michigan and Minnesota were two football programs that were heading in different directions during the Carr Era. Michigan was ranked in all eleven of the games that they played against Minnesota. The Gophers were only ranked in two games (2003 and 2004). Of course, every game was a sellout in Ann Arbor, but not so much in Minneapolis.

Coach Carr won five of the six games played in Michigan Stadium. Lloyd won once against Jim Wacker and won three of the four games that he coached against Glen Mason in the Big House. Mason's unranked Gophers defeated Carr's Wolverines by three points (23-20) for Lloyd's only loss to the Gophers.

Coach Carr won his only game against Tim Brewster at Michigan Stadium in 2007. Lloyd Carr's teams scored an average of just over thirty-one points per game against the Gophers in Ann Arbor and allowed just over fourteen points per game for a difference of over sixteen points (+16.8) per game. Lloyd Carr had a lot of success when he coached at the Big House and his body of work against Minnesota contributed to his exceptional home record.

Things always ended well for Michigan when they played in Minnesota. The Wolverines won all five games in Minneapolis. Carr finished with five road wins against the Gophers—one against Jim Wacker and four against Glen Mason. Carr's biggest comeback win took place in 2003 when his twentieth ranked Wolverines "upset" the seventeenth ranked Golden Gophers by three points (38-35). Michigan trailed the whole game. Carr's team was down by twenty-one points at the end of the third quarter (28-7). The Wolverines put the pedal to the metal and scored thirty-one points in the fourth quarter to win it. This was even better than Carr's comeback win in his first game in 1995 and is still the biggest comeback victory in Michigan football history.

Here is a breakdown of the key statistics for the Michigan vs Minnesota series during the Lloyd Carr Era from 1995 to 2007:

Games	W-L-T	Scored/Avg.	Allowed/Avg.	+/- Difference
Home	5-1	188/31.3	87/14.5	+16.8
Road	5-0	128/25.6	58/11.6	+14.0
Totals	**10-1**	**316/28.7**	**145/13.2**	**+15.5**

Overall, Coach Carr's teams won ten games and lost one game against Minnesota. He finished with a record of two wins and no losses against Jim Wacker, seven wins and one loss against Glen Mason and one win and no losses against Tim Brewster.

The "jug" only left Ann Arbor once in Carr's tenure. Coach Carr's teams were solid on both sides of the ball in the series as they averaged over twenty-eight points per game (28.7) and allowed only thirteen points per game (13.2).

The odds were pretty good that the Wolverines would win by a couple touchdowns when they faced the Gophers during the Lloyd Carr Era.

Michigan vs Minnesota Series Summary

Michigan and Minnesota played a total of eleven games during the Lloyd Carr Era. The Wolverines improved their series advantage by winning ten of those eleven contests. Carr's only loss was in 2005 when Michigan posted a disappointing record of 7 wins and 5 losses.

The chart below shows what the Michigan vs. Minnesota football series looked like before Lloyd Carr became the head coach. It also ws what he did during his tenure. Finally, the bottom line shows what the rivalry looked like when Coach Carr hung up his whistle in 2007. It is an interesting chart.

Time Period	Won-Lost-Tied	Win %	Michigan Advantage
1892-1994	59-23-3	.711	+36 wins
1995-2007	10-1-0	.909	+9 wins
1892-2007	69-24-3	.734	+45 wins

At the end of the 2007 season the series totals looked pretty familiar. Michigan and Minnesota had battled ninety-six times and Michigan had posted sixty-nine wins, twenty-four losses, and three ties. Under Lloyd Carr's leadership, the Wolverines increased their winning percentage against Minnesota from just over seventy-one percent to seventy-three percent. Michigan also increased their "win" advantage to forty-five thanks to Carr's dominance over the Gophers. The Wolverines remained in full control of the Michigan vs. Minnesota football series and the Little Brown Jug when Lloyd Carr retired after the 2007 football season.

Michigan vs. Minnesota Program Comparisons 1995-2007

Yes, Michigan and Minnesota have been playing football against each other since 1892. Both programs have winning traditions but Michigan has won a lot more than Minnesota. Of course, the Wolverines have won more games than any other program so it's not something that the Gophers should be ashamed of.

With Lloyd Carr at the helm, the Wolverines continued to post numbers that were much more impressive than those totaled by the Gophers. At the end of the 2007 season, the Michigan football program claimed 869 total wins while Minnesota totaled 627 program victories.

It is easy to see why the Wolverines were able to increase their advantage over the Gophers when you look at the numbers on the chart on the next page. Coach Carr inherited a strong program from Bo Schembechler and Gary Moeller—and he kept it going! The Michigan football program continued to be one of the best in the country while Minnesota struggled during the Lloyd Carr Era. Minnesota had three head coaches from 1995 to 2007 while Michigan had just one. Yes, winning is good for coaching careers and program stability. Michigan had both from 1995 to 2007 and Minnesota did not.

Once again, I used a revealing chart to compare the performance of the Wolverines and Gophers from 1995 to 2007. As you can see, Michigan had the advantage in all the "good" numbers and Minnesota did not. Lloyd Carr's tenure in Ann Arbor was good for Wolverine players and fans. The numbers displayed below show that Michigan was a lot better than Minnesota from 1995 to 2007—period!

Statistical Area	**Michigan**	**Minnesota**
Total Wins	122	72
Total Losses	40	84
Winning Percentage	.753	.462
Winning Seasons	13	5
Losing Seasons	0	7
Even Seasons	0	1
National Championships	1	0
Top Ten Poll Rankings	6	0
Heisman Trophy Winners	1	0
All-American Selections*	12	4

*Consensus All-Americans

CHAPTER 20

A Closer Look: Coach Carr vs. Ohio State

The Michigan vs. Ohio State rivalry reached new levels of intensity and national interest by the time that Bo turned the program over to Gary Moeller. Fortunately for Wolverine fans, Michigan was on a roll against Ohio State in 1990. Not only that, but Bo, the first Michigan Coach to be born in Ohio, was giving the reins to a former Buckeye player who happened to be a co-captain for Woody Hayes in 1963. When Gary Moeller coached his first game against Ohio State, he had played in three games against Michigan as a player (all victories) and eighteen games (9-8-1) as an assistant coach under Bo. Mo's twenty-one years' worth of experience paid dividends for the Wolverines starting in 1990.

Michigan vs. Ohio State: The Carr Era 1995-2007

Lloyd Carr knew about the Michigan rivalry with that school down south. He joined Bo's staff in 1980 and had fifteen of these high-profile contests under his belt. Ten of those games were with Bo and the record was six wins and four losses. Five of the games were with Mo and the record against the Buckeyes was three wins, one loss and one tie. Carr knew about the pressures involved in this game. He was aware of the intense preparation that it took to play in the greatest rivalry in college football. Now, it was his turn to lead his team against OSU.

Both programs continued to win at impressive rates at the start of the Lloyd Carr Era. Against John Cooper, Lloyd Carr won at a slightly higher rate in all games during this era and had a slightly better record in conference play. The really good news for the Wolverines was that Carr won five of the six games that he coached against the Buckeyes when John Cooper was on the sidelines.

Lloyd Carr also managed to win the overall competition for Big Ten Championships against John Cooper. Carr won three (1997, 1998, and 2000) while Cooper managed to win two (1996 and 1998). That is about as competitive as two rival coaches can be.

Image 25: Lloyd Carr's first six games against John Cooper and Ohio State ended well since Michigan posted 5 wins and only 1 loss. Then, the tide changed. Permission: Bentley Historical Library, University of Michigan.

Things changed when Jim Tressel arrived in Columbus. Both programs were still winning a ton of games, but the Buckeyes won nine more overall and one more in the Big Ten Conference.

The bad news for the Wolverines was that Carr lost six of seven games to Tressel and Ohio State. He also came up short in Big Ten Championships against Tressel and his teams. Carr won two (2003 and 2004) while Tressel won four (2002, 2005, 2006, 2007). Things were still competitive, but Ohio State and Jim Tressel held the upper hand in the latter part of the Lloyd Carr Era.

Now, it is time to take a closer look at the key statistics for the Michigan vs. Ohio State series during Lloyd Carr's tenure. How many games did he win at home and away against the hated Buckeyes?

Lloyd Carr won four games and lost three in his Buckeye duels at Michigan Stadium. He won all three games home games against John Cooper, but only won one game in four tries against Tressel in Ann Arbor. Carr's Wolverines scored an average of twenty-five points per game against Cooper's teams and only allowed eighteen, which gave him the winning margin in all three games. Carr's teams scored just over nineteen points against Tressel's Buckeyes, but allowed nineteen points so that explains why things didn't go so well for the Wolverines at home from 2001 to 2007.

Coach Carr vs. OSU Summary 1995 to 2007

Michigan and Ohio State played thirteen games during the Lloyd Carr Era. The Wolverines lost some ground to the Buckeyes from 1995 to 2007. Coach Carr's started strong against OSU but didn't finish that way. After winning five of his six games, he lost six of the last seven. Overall, Coach Carr posted a final record of 6 wins and 7 losses against Ohio State.

Games	W-L-T	Scored/Avg.	Allowed/Avg.	+/-
Home	4-3-0	154/22.0	140/20	+2.0
Road	2-4-0	136/22.6	159/26.5	-3.9
Totals	6-7-0	290/22.3	299/23.0	-.7

Things never seemed to go as planned when Lloyd Carr took his teams to Columbus, Ohio. He started strong since he won two of his first three games in "The Horseshoe" against John Cooper. Carr's Wolverines scored sixty-seven points in those three games and allowed sixty-six so he was very fortunate to come away with two wins. Unfortunately, Lloyd Carr did not win a game in Columbus once Jim Tressel arrived. He lost all three games, but two of the three were close (14-9 in 2002 and 42-39 in 2006).

During his tenure, Lloyd Carr coached in some classic Wolverine versus Buckeye battles. Three of the games were top five match ups starting in 1997 when number one Michigan defeated number four OSU by six points (20-14). The second top five game was played in 2003 when the fifth ranked Wolverines knocked off the fourth ranked Buckeyes by fourteen points (35-21). The first and only "#1 vs. #2" match-up between number one (OSU) and number two (Michigan) took place in 2006. The Buckeyes won a shootout by three points (42-39) the day after the death of Bo Schembechler. There were lots of great games during the Carr Era, but these three stood out.

The annual battle for border bragging rights and Big Ten Championships continued to make for great college football drama between these historic rivals from 1995 to 2007. Coach Lloyd Carr's teams won six games and lost seven to the hated Buckeyes during his tenure.

Lloyd Carr finished with a record of five wins and one loss against John Cooper. I am certain that he was sad to see "Coop" leave Columbus. Lloyd Carr was only able to defeat Jim Tressel once in seven contests. Tressel beat him three times in Ann Arbor and three times in Columbus. Yes, it really got ugly towards the end. Most of the games were close, but each coach did gain one double digit win.

Michigan vs. Ohio State Series Summary

The chart below shows what the Michigan vs. Ohio State football series looked like before Lloyd Carr became the head coach. It also shows what he did during his tenure. Finally, the bottom line shows what the rivalry looked like when Coach Carr hung up his whistle in 2007. It is an interesting look at the history between these rivals.

Time Period	Won-Lost-Tied	Win %	Michigan Advantage
1897-1994	51-34-6	.593	+17 wins
1995-2007	6-7-0	.462	-1 win
1897-2007	57-41-6	.577	+16 wins

At the end of the 2007 season the Michigan vs. Ohio State football series was tighter than ever as the Buckeyes gained ground. Michigan and Ohio State had now played each other a total of one hundred and four times. Michigan still held the advantage in the series with fifty-seven wins, forty-one losses and six ties. However, Michigan's overall winning percentage against the Buckeyes dropped from just under sixty-percent (.593) to just under fifty-eight (.577). Jim Tressel really changed the series for the worse for Wolverine fans.

Michigan vs. Ohio State Program Comparisons 1995-2007

Lloyd Carr's tenure had a lot of good news and a little bad news. The good news was that his 122 victories kept Michigan at the top of college football's all-time winning list with 869 program victories. The bad news was that Ohio State won 130 games during the same time period. However, OSU still trailed Michigan by seventy-one (71) wins in the chase for the most victories in college football history.

Here is how both programs compared from 1995 to 2007:

Statistical Area	Michigan	Ohio State
Total Wins	122	130
Total Losses	40	31
Winning Percentage	.753	.807
Winning Seasons	13	12
Losing Seasons	0	0
Even Seasons	0	1
National Championships	1	1
Top Ten Poll Rankings	6	8
Heisman Trophy Winners	1	2
All-American Selections*	12	20

*Consensus All-Americans

Michigan continued to have the most wins in college football history at the end of the 2007 season. Lloyd Carr's twenty-eight-year coaching run in Ann Arbor was over. Ohio State closed the gap between them and the Wolverines by eight (8) program wins from 1995 to 2007. Michigan was very good during the Lloyd Carr Era. Unfortunately for Wolverine fans, the Buckeyes were a little bit better.

CHAPTER 21

A Closer Look: Coach Carr vs. Michigan State

The Michigan vs. Michigan State rivalry was as intense as it had ever been when Bo put Mo in charge of the Michigan football program. The games were starting to take on a nasty edge as the Spartans were tired of getting kicked around by the Wolverines. Michigan State fans were happy to see Bo Schembechler retire at the end of the 1989 season. He won seventeen of twenty-one games against the Spartans. Everyone in East Lansing hoped that things would be better when Gary Moeller took over. Things did get a little better since Mo won three games and lost two games to MSU. The big question in Ann Arbor in 1995 was, "How would things go in the series with Lloyd Carr at the helm?"

Once again, the level of intensity in the Wolverine versus Spartans rivalry requires a closer look at everything. I will draw comparisons of the overall records, conference records, the head-to-head matchups, and Big Ten Championships won during Coach Carr's tenure. Things just matter a little more in great rivalries, so we have to look a little deeper to find out how the coaches and the programs were doing in the Carr Era. Now, it's time to take a closer look at what happened between Lloyd Carr and Michigan State from 1995 to 2007.

Image 26: The Paul Bunyan Trophy showed up with Governor G. Mennen Williams at the first Big Ten football game between UM and MSU in 1953. The hated rivals now had a trophy to contend for, not just "Bragging Rights." Fritz Crisler didn't think much about the trophy since he had it stored in a closet the first time Michigan won it. Today, all Wolverines want it to remain in Ann Arbor as much as possible. Permission: Bentley Historical Library, University of Michigan.

Michigan vs. Michigan State: The Carr Era 1995-2007

Lloyd Carr knew just about everything there was to know about the Michigan vs. Michigan State rivalry when he took over in 1995. He had been through fifteen of these games as a member of Bo (10) and Mo's (5) staffs from 1980 to 1994. He was on the sidelines for eleven wins and endured four losses to the hated Spartans. Coach Moeller won three of his last four contests against MSU. Lloyd Carr wanted to keep that trend going. Coach Carr also knew a lot about the Paul Bunyan Trophy. Although he thought it was "the ugliest trophy in college football" he wanted it in the Michigan locker room after every game against Michigan State.

By the time Lloyd Carr took charge in Ann Arbor in 1995, both programs were heading in completely different directions. Michigan was winning over seventy percent of their games and competing for the conference championship almost every year. Sadly, the Spartans struggled to win half of their games. Michigan State went through four coaches during the Carr Era. The Spartans were doing everything they could to compete against Michigan but it wasn't really working.

Coach Carr vs. MSU Coaches 1995-2007

Lloyd Carr probably had no idea how many times he would face a new coach when he squared off against Nick Saban and his Spartans in 1995. The MSU job became a revolving door as the Spartan administration struggled to find someone who could re-create a winning football tradition at Michigan State. While stability was lacking in East Lansing, the Wolverines kept rolling along in Ann Arbor. Bottom line—Lloyd Carr out-performed everyone that the Spartans threw at him from 1995 to 2007

Lloyd Carr's first game against Michigan State did not go well since he lost to another series first-timer named Nick Saban. The Spartans upset the Wolverines by a score of 28 to 25.

Things went better since Coach Carr won the next three games. Saban won the last game and then he went to LSU. Good riddance Nick! Carr and Saban matched up five times between 1995 and 1999.

Here is what Carr's final record against Nick Saban looked like:

Games	Won-Lost	Win %	Scored/Avg.	Allowed	+/-
5	3-2	.600	153/30.6	115/23.0	+7.6

Bobby Williams turned out to be Lloyd Carr's next coaching adversary in East Lansing after Saban skipped town. Carr won the first game in 2000 and the last game in 2002. Williams won in 2001 when his unranked Spartans upset #6 Michigan in East Lansing by a score of 26-24. Carr's last win against Williams was a dominating victory (49-3). Unfortunately, Coach Williams was fired the next day.

Lloyd Carr's final record against Bobby Williams looked like this in 2002:

Games	Won-Lost	Win %	Scored/Avg.	Allowed	+/-
3	2-1	.667	87.0/29.0	29/9.7	+19.3

John L. Smith was the next man up in East Lansing in 2003. Even though he was an "outsider" Smith quickly learned about the intense rivalry between the two schools. The good news for MSU fans was that Coach Smith always had his team ready for the Wolverines. The bad news was that his team could never beat the hated Maize and Blue football team. Michigan won all four games including a 31-13 victory in 2006. Fortunately for Coach Carr, he ended the intense series on a winning note. John Smith did not since he was fired at the end of the 2006 season.

Here is what Lloyd Carr's final record against John L. Smith looked like in 2006:

Games	Won-Lost	Win %	Scored/Avg.	Allowed	+/-
4	4-0	1.000	137/34.3	101/25.3	+9.0

Mark Dantonio was the fourth, and last, coach that Lloyd Carr faced at Michigan State. Coach Dantonio knew a lot about the intense football rivalry between Michigan and Michigan State.

Mark Dantonio was an assistant coach in East Lansing from 1995 to 2000. He left MSU to become the Defensive Coordinator at Ohio State from 2001 to 2003. Then, he was the head coach at Cincinnati for three years (2004-2006). Dantonio came to East Lansing with a chip on his shoulder. He was on a mission to beat Michigan and earn respect for Michigan State football.

Mark Dantonio and his Spartans were ready for Lloyd Carr's Wolverines in 2007. Unranked Michigan State led for most of the game before losing a heartbreaker (28-24) to Michigan. Of course, this is the game that Mike Hart dropped the "Little Brother" comment on Dantonio and Spartan Nation.

Whoa, the intensity level of the Michigan vs. Michigan State rivalry went up about five notches after that game. Lloyd Carr was probably happy to leave East Lansing with a win in 2007.

Lloyd Carr and Mark Dantonio only coached against each other in one very exciting game. Fortunately for Carr, he posted a perfect record of 1 win and 0 losses.

Game	Won-Lost	Win %	Scored/Avg.	Allowed	+/-
1	1-0	1.000	28/28.0	24/24.0	+4.0

Coach Carr vs. Michigan State – Final Record from 1995-2007

Lloyd Carr was perfect at Michigan Stadium in the six games that his Wolverines hosted the Spartans. None of the games were really close since his team scored an average of over thirty-five points per game and only allowed about sixteen points per contest.

On average, Carr's teams were nineteen points better than Michigan State when they played in the Big House. Statistics like that make it hard to lose to anybody. The Spartans didn't have a coach in this era that could steal a victory from the Wolverines in Ann Arbor.

Things were different when the Wolverines traveled to East Lansing from 1995 to 2007. Michigan still had the advantage since they won 4 games and lost 3 games in Spartan Stadium. However, the Wolverines were only about three points better (3.1) than the Spartans in seven games in East Lansing. Yes, just about every game in Spartan Stadium was a nail biter.

Games	W-L-T	Scored/Avg.	Allowed/Avg.	+/- Difference
Home	6-0-0	213/35.5	99/16.5	+19.0
Road	4-3-0	192/27.4	170/24.3	+3.1
Totals	**10-3-0**	**405/31.1**	**269/20.6**	**+10.5**

Michigan was ranked in eleven of the thirteen games played in the Carr Era while the Spartans were only ranked four times during this period. Only three of the games (1997, 1999, and 2003) featured ranked Wolverine and Spartan teams. Neither rival was ranked in 1998 when they faced off in Ann Arbor. However, it didn't matter since the Wolverines earned a twelve-point victory (29-17). The highest ranked game occurred in 1999 when third ranked Michigan traveled to East Lansing. The eleventh ranked Spartans shocked the Wolverines with a 34-31 upset victory.

In the all-important category of Big Ten Championships, Lloyd Carr held a big edge over the Spartans. His teams won five Big Ten Titles but the Spartans did not win any. Carr's teams won championships in 1997, 1998, 2000, 2003 and 2004. Coach Carr compiled a very impressive body of work against the Spartans from 1995 to 2007. He was able to dominate the State of Michigan and return the Wolverines to a place that Bo Schembechler had journeyed to during his tenure.

Michigan vs. Michigan State Series Summary 1995 to 2007

Michigan and Michigan State played every season from 1995 to 2007. Unlike Notre Dame and Minnesota, this game is always a part of any college football season. Lloyd Carr lost his first game to the Spartans just like Bo and Mo did. Then, he took charge of the series and won ten of the next twelve games.

Once again, the chart below shows what the Michigan vs. Michigan State football series looked like before Lloyd Carr became the head coach. It also shows what he did during his tenure. Finally, the bottom line shows what the rivalry looked like when Coach Carr hung up his whistle in 2007. Lloyd Carr continued Michigan's winning tradition against Michigan State and always found a place for what he called "The Ugliest Trophy" in college football."

Time Period	Won-Lost-Tied	Win %	Michigan Advantage
1896-1994	57-25-5	.683	+32 wins
1995-2007	10-3-0	.909	+7 wins
1896-2007	67-28-5	.695	+39 wins

Michigan and Michigan State continued to be hated and heated rivals during the Lloyd H. Carr Era. The games always had an extra edge that bordered on "nasty" because Michigan had been so dominant for so many years. Sparty was getting tired of being the "Little Brother" and the "second" football team in the state. The Wolverines gained some additional ground against the Spartans during this era. I'm sure that Michigan State fans were glad to see Coach Lloyd Carr retire in 2007.

At the end of the 2007 season, Michigan's series lead was still significant. Michigan and Michigan State had played exactly one hundred games. The Wolverines still held a big advantage in the series with sixty-seven wins, twenty-eight losses and five ties (67-28-5). Coach Lloyd Carr increased Michigan's winning percentage against the Spartans from just over sixty-eight (.683) in 1994 to almost seventy-percent (.695) by the end of the 2007 season.

Michigan vs. Michigan State Program Comparisons 1995-2007

Here is how both programs compared from 1995 to 2007:

Statistical Area	Michigan	Michigan State
Total Wins	122	80
Total Losses	40	75
Winning Percentage	.753	1
Winning Seasons	13	6
Losing Seasons	0	5
Even Seasons	0	2
National Championships	1	0
Top Ten Poll Rankings	6	1
Heisman Trophy Winners	1	0
All-American Selections*	12	2

*Consensus All-Americans

Lloyd Carr faced four different men from Michigan State who tried to challenge him and his Wolverines for football supremacy in the Great Lakes State. They all failed, which is why Carr coached for thirteen years. No Spartan football coach lasted longer than four years. Lloyd Carr had his football team in position to challenge for the Big Ten Championship almost every season. Unfortunately, the same could not be said for Michigan State. The Spartans seemed to be starting over every three to four years while the Wolverines just kept rolling along.

There is nothing better in college football than rivalry games. Michigan has more rivals than anybody and that's what makes coaching the Wolverines so challenging and so rewarding. Everybody wants to beat the winningest team in college football. It has been that way for a very long time and will continue to be that way in the foreseeable future.

A Final Look at Coach Carr and the Big Four – 1995 to 2007

Again, rivalry games are the best ones to win and the hardest ones to lose. Each contest only counts as one victory or one defeat, but those rival wins are a little sweeter for the victor and the rival losses are just a lot tougher on the losing team. That's just the way it is and that is what makes the rival games so special. Began

Now it is time to take a final look at Coach Carr's efforts against the "Big Four." Overall, Lloyd Carr produced some excellent results against Michigan's rivals during his tenure. He posted winning records against Notre Dame, Minnesota, and Michigan State. Unfortunately, his fast start against Ohio State fizzled over the last four years of his time at Michigan.

Team	Games	Won-Lost-Tied	Win %
Notre Dame	9	5-4-0	.560
Minnesota	11	10-1-0	.910
Ohio State	13	6-7-0	.460
Michigan State	13	10-3-0	.770
Totals	**46**	**31-15-0**	**.674**

Coach Lloyd Carr's thirteen-year tenure was the third longest head coaching run in Michigan football history. When he called it quits after the 2007 season, only the legendary Fielding H. Yost (25 years) and his mentor/friend Bo Schembechler (21 years) stayed on the sidelines longer than Coach Lloyd Carr. His overall performance against Michigan's biggest rivals was laudable. His winning percentage of just over sixty-seven percent (.674) wasn't that far behind the winning rates that Schembechler and Moeller posted before him.

A Final Report on Coach Carr's Former and Potential Employers

In addition to Michigan's four traditional rivals, Lloyd Carr had three other teams that he coached against that had a little more meaning than most games on a Wolverine football schedule. Yes, Eastern Michigan, Illinois, and Wisconsin all generated some extra attention and emotion when they faced Coach Lloyd Carr and his Wolverines from 1995 to 2007.

Lloyd Carr began his college coaching career at Eastern Michigan in Ypsilanti, Michigan. He was the defensive backs coach from 1976 to 1977. His tenure at EMU was short but eventful. He loved being a full-time coach at the college level and he learned a lot from Ed Cheblek and other assistant coaches like Gerry DiNardo, who became a long-time friend of Lloyd Carr. Although he left Ypsilanti on good terms, Carr showed no loyalty to EMU when he became a head coach at Michigan.

Michigan played three games against Eastern Michigan during Coach Carr's tenure in Ann Arbor. The first game was played in 1998 and the Wolverines won by a score of 59-20. Game number two took place in 2005 and it went badly for Eagles since they lost to the Wolverines by a score of 55-0. Lloyd Carr continued to dominate his former employer in 2007 with a 33-22 victory in the Big House. Of course, Michigan was favored to win every game against the Eagles and that's exactly what happened. Whatever good feelings Lloyd Carr had about his time at Eastern Michigan did not affect the way he coached against his former team. It wasn't personal, it was just football business.

Lloyd Carr's second coaching job was at the University of Illinois in Champaign, Illinois. He was hired to coach defensive backs for second year head coach Gary Moeller in 1978. Lloyd Carr served on Moeller's staff for two seasons. Unfortunately, Illinois did not win enough games from 1977 to 1979. Everyone was fired at the end of the 1979 season. As it turned out, Moeller and Carr ended up in Ann Arbor in 1980 and Illinois had three enemies. Bo Schembechler always enjoyed a win over Illinois and so did Gary Moeller and Lloyd Carr.

During his head coaching career, Coach Carr faced Illinois nine times from 1995 to 2007. He posted a final record of 8 wins and 1 loss against the program that fired him in 1979. I think Lloyd Carr always got a little more "fired-up" for a game against the Fighting Illini than most teams on a Michigan football schedule. What do you think?

And that leaves me with one more team that was "special" to Coach Lloyd Carr. As I mentioned earlier, Carr applied for the head coaching vacancy at the University of Wisconsin in 1989. I don't know who else applied for the job but I know that Lloyd Carr did not get the job. Instead, Barry Alvarez, Notre Dame's Defensive Coordinator was hired to lead the Badger football program. Coach Alvarez did an outstanding job of energizing and rebuilding the Wisconsin football program. He won two Big Ten Titles and led the Badgers to two Rose Bowl wins. Barry Alvarez retired after sixteen years as the longest tenured head coach in Wisconsin football history. He was also the winningest Badger football coach ever. Yes, he did very well.

However, there was one thing that Coach Alvarez did not do very well which was beat Michigan when Lloyd Carr was there from 1995 to 2007. Coach Carr coached nine games against Barry Alvarez and won seven. Lloyd Carr's winning percentage against the Badgers was almost seventy-eight percent (.778). Oh, by the way, Coach Carr won five Big Ten Championships and one national championship during his tenure at Michigan. Yes, I think that Wisconsin and Barry Alvarez were two rivals that got Coach Carr's juices going a little more than most teams in the Big Ten Conference.

Coach Lloyd Carr was hired to win as many games as he and his teams could possibly win during his thirteen years in Ann Arbor. I am certain he prepared himself, his staff, and his players to win every game. Of course, that didn't happen because it is impossible to win every time and all the time. Well Coach Carr didn't win them all but he won a lot of games from 1995 to 2007. I know that he wanted to beat every team on the Michigan schedule for thirteen seasons. I also know that Notre Dame, Minnesota, Ohio State, Michigan State, Illinois and Wisconsin were teams that he wanted to beat for all of the reasons I have mentioned in this chapter.

CHAPTER 22

A Closer Look: Coach Carr and Michigan Stadium

The Michigan Wolverines have been one of the leaders in college football attendance ever since Fielding Yost built Michigan Stadium in 1927. It is a wonderful thing to have a football stadium that can hold eighty-thousand or more people. Of course, it is problematic if you don't have the fans paying to sit in the seats and the finances to keep everything going. Fortunately, Fielding Yost and Fritz Crisler were successful at selling lots of tickets to Michigan football games for a very long time. Unfortunately, attendance was slipping in Ann Arbor in 1968 and so were the revenues. It didn't take new Athletic Director Don Canham long to figure out that he had to find a way to fill Michigan Stadium and pay for Crisler Arena. He had a lot of bills to pay and thirty-thousand empty seats for most games was not helping him balance the Athletic Department's expanding and demanding budget.

As a matter of fact, the Wolverines were only averaging about seventy-percent of their capacity for football attendance when Mr. Canham arrived in 1968. The Wolverines were not winning enough games and it was getting harder to pay the bills. In time, Mr. Canham solved Michigan's football attendance and revenue problems. Michigan took the national attendance lead from Ohio State in 1974 when the average attendance spiked from 85,024 in 1973 to 93,684. The Wolverines increased their attendance numbers again in 1975 to over 98,000 per game and then hit an average of over 103,159 per game in 1976. Michigan has averaged over 100,000 people per game every year since 1976.

Crowds in excess of one hundred thousand people were the norm in 1995. Of course, a winning program was at the center of it all. Wolverine fans were coming to Michigan Stadium in record numbers. The transition from a seventy percent "fill rate" to over one hundred percent of capacity for every game created a significant funding stream for the Michigan Athletic Department. Wolverine football was generating millions of dollars. That money was needed to fund the ever-expanding Wolverine sports empire. Women's sports continued to grow, which meant that they needed funds and facilities to compete at the expected level for Wolverine sports. If Lloyd Carr continued to win like Bo and Mo, Michigan fans would come by the hundreds of thousands. So, that's what Coach Carr focused on—winning football games and sending Wolverine fans home happy, most of the time!

Coach Carr's Adventures in the Big House 1995 to 2007

Lloyd Carr stepped into one of the biggest jobs in college football with his eyes wide open. He had a clear understanding of the expectations that came with Michigan football—both on the field and off. He probably didn't want Mo to leave, but Carr was ready to step up when he was asked. In May 1995, Joe Roberson asked and the rest is history. The "interim" coach became a Michigan football legend who didn't lose very often at Michigan Stadium. At one point he won sixteen straight games in the Big House. However, when he did lose it was usually a memorable event in Michigan football history but not always. Let's take a closer look at some of the big wins and disappointing losses that helped define Coach Carr's thirteen-year tenure at Michigan.

Coach Carr's Notable Home Victories:

- First win & smallest margin of victory: 18-17 win over Virginia in August 1995
- First Conference & Homecoming Win: 52-17 over Minnesota in October 1995
- First Shutout Win: 5-0 over November 1995
- Biggest Upset Win: #18 UM defeated #2 OSU by a score of 31-23 in November 1995
- Most Important Home Win: 20-14 over OSU in November 1997 To clinch first Big Ten Conference Championship
- 800th win in Michigan football history on September 30, 2000 against Wisconsin (13-10).
- Biggest Conference & Homecoming Win: 58-0 over Minnesota in October 2000
- First Overtime Win: 27-24 over Penn State in October 2002
- Last win over OSU: 35-21 in November 2003
- First, and only, triple overtime win (45-37) against Michigan State on October 30, 2004
- Biggest Non-Conference Win: 55-0 over Eastern Michigan in September 2005
- Longest Home Win Streak: 16 games from November 2002 to September 2005
- 850th win in Michigan football history on September 2, 2000 against Vanderbilt (27-7).

Coach Carr's Notable Home Losses:

- First Loss & First Conference Loss: 19-13 to Northwestern in October 1995
- Biggest Conference & Homecoming Loss: 34-9 to Iowa on October 26, 2002
- Longest Home Losing Streak: 2 games (Appalachian State and Oregon) in Sep 2007
- Biggest Upset Loss: 34-32 to Appalachian State in September 2007
- Biggest home loss: 39-7 to Oregon—September 2007

Image 27: Michigan Stadium was "Home Sweet Home" for Coach Carr and his Wolverines from 1995 to 2007. Photo from the Barry Gallagher Family Collection.

There were many keys to Lloyd Carr's success at Michigan Stadium, but it really was pretty simple. His teams had double digit point differentials every year except for 1996 and 2002. Coach Carr never had less than an eight-point edge against his football guests on average. Carr's best year was 2003 when his Wolverines won all seven home games by just over thirty-one points per game—wow! The numbers were pretty good in 2000 as well when Michigan won by an average of twenty-seven points in the Big House.

Coach Carr's Michigan Stadium Data Report - 1995-2007*

Games	W-L	Average	% Capacity	Scored	Allowed	+/-
86	74-12	109,414	102.8	30.1	14.8	+15.3

Note-Michigan Stadium capacity was 102,501 from 1995 to 1997. It increased to 107,501 from 1998 to 2007.

Lloyd Carr had a winning home record in every one of the thirteen seasons that he coached in the Big House. He had five perfect seasons, six seasons with only one loss, and only two seasons (2003 and 2007) with three home losses. Coach Carr's Wolverines won sixteen straight home games between 2002 and 2005. They also reeled off thirteen consecutive home wins from 1999 to 2001. His teams did not lose consecutive home games until 2007 when they opened the season with losses to Appalachian State and Oregon.

Overall, Lloyd Carr's teams averaged just over thirty points per game and allowed just under fifteen during his thirteen-year tenure. Coach Carr's positive point differential of over fifteen points per game (+15.3) allowed the fans and the odds makers to count on a victory at Michigan Stadium when Lloyd Carr was coaching. Coach Carr's defenses posted seven shutouts in front of the home fans. On the offensive side, Lloyd Carr's teams scored at least six points in every game in the Big House and never endured a shutout loss at home from 1995 to 2007.

Attendance was never a problem during the Lloyd Carr Era. Michigan fans supported Carr's Wolverines in record numbers. Carr's teams attracted many record crowds and helped keep Michigan at the top of the college football attendance rankings. The "average" crowd for a Lloyd Carr coached team at the Big House was over one hundred and nine thousand fans per game (109,414). Again, every crowd was in excess of one hundred thousand people and the only question was "How much over capacity will attendance be today?"

Lloyd Carr's teams won just over eighty-six percent (.869) of their home games from 1995 to 2007. That winning rate helped fuel attendance numbers that were the best in the nation for every season but one. In 1997 his Wolverines won every game and finished with two of the three national championship trophies. However, they did lose one competition, but it wasn't on the field.

Michigan finished second to the University of Tennessee in national attendance by an average margin of ninety fans per game. Both teams averaged over one hundred and six thousand fans per game, but the Volunteers came in a little bit higher than the Wolverines (106,538 people per game versus 106,448). Michigan knew that the Volunteers were expanding Nehlen Stadium to a capacity which would eclipse the capacity of Michigan Stadium. Michigan went to work as quickly as they could but could not move fast enough to keep the Volunteers from claiming the top spot in college football attendance for the 1997 season. When construction was finished in 1998, Michigan had increased its capacity by five thousand seats (from 102,501 to 107,501) and that was the last time anyone came close to beating Michigan in average attendance.

Coach Carr and Homecoming – 1995 to 2007

The Michigan homecoming tradition has been going strong in Ann Arbor since 1897. Lloyd Carr was given the chance to do things his way when he was named "interim" head coach at Michigan. Of course, "his way" was strongly influenced by what his mentors, Bo Schembechler and Gary Moeller, did when he was serving on their staffs. Lloyd was involved in many of Bo's homecoming victories and all of Mo's homecoming games. It would be interesting to see how he handled things on that special football Saturday.

Coach Carr's homecoming resume began with a seven-game winning streak. Every game was a double-digit victory margin, except a seven-point win (27-20) over Indiana in 1996. Carr's first homecoming loss (2002) wasn't even close as Iowa won by twenty-five points (34-9) and left Lloyd Carr wondering about what just happened to his eighth ranked Wolverines. Lloyd Carr's biggest homecoming win was a blowout/shutout of Indiana (58-0) in 2000. He also had two other games that saw his Wolverines score over fifty points and one more where they totaled forty-eight.

Carr's Wolverines generally played very well on Homecoming Day which allowed their coach to post eleven victories in thirteen games. They scored an average of about thirty-two points (32.4) per game and only allowed about fifteen points (14.7) per game to the visitors on this special Michigan football day.

His winning rate on homecoming day was just over eighty-four percent (.846) which is right up there with the best ever.

Homecoming Data Report – 1990- 2010

Coach	Games	W-L	Win %	Scored/Avg.	Allowed/Avg.	+/-
Carr	13	11-2	.846	421/32.4	191/14.7	+17.7

Coach Carr's teams were almost eighteen points better (17.7) on homecoming which is why they were so successful in these special games on the Michigan Football Schedule from 1995 to 2007.

Summary: Michigan's Home Winning Tradition Continued

The chart below takes a closer look at all the coaches who coached in Michigan Stadium from 1927 through 2007. As you can see, those coaches won a lot of games in "The Big House."

Years	Coach	Games	W-L-T	Win %
1927-1928	Wieman	11	7-4-0	.636
1929-1937	Kipke	50	30-16-4	.640
1938-1947	Crisler	57	46-8-3	.833
1948-1958	Oosterbaan	67	46-19-2	.701
1958-1968	Elliott	61	33-26-2	.557
1969-1989	Schembechler	134	115-16-3	.869
1990-1994	Moeller	31	22-8-1	.726
1995-2007	Carr	86	74-12-0	.860
1927-2007	Eight Coaches	499	376-108-15	.768

Coaches Tad Wieman and Harry Kipke had winning records in Michigan Stadium. Fritz Crisler set the bar very high for every coach who followed him since he won almost just over eighty-three percent (.833) of his home games. Unfortunately, Bennie Oosterbaan and Bump Elliott did not come close to Crisler's winning rate.

Then, Bo Schembechler arrived and really raised the bar. By the time he left, Bo was the only Wolverine football coach to win over one hundred games in Michigan Stadium. He also surpassed Crisler's achievement by winning almost eight-seven percent (.869) of his games in "The Big House."

Coach Lloyd Carr learned some important lessons from his mentor Bo Schembechler. One lesson was how to win a lot of games in Michigan Stadium. Bo was the best there ever was at the Big House, but Lloyd Carr finished right behind him in the end. When Lloyd Carr retired, he had a record of seventy-four wins and twelve losses. His winning rate at the "Big House" was eighty-six percent (.860). Bo finished with a home winning rate of almost eight-seven percent (.869). The difference between the two winningest coaches in Michigan Stadium history was pretty insignificant (.009). Bo was the best at Michigan Stadium but Lloyd Carr was right behind him! I know that Coach Carr feels no shame in being second place on the all-time winning list at Michigan Stadium. No shame at all!

Lloyd Carr's teams posted five undefeated home seasons in thirteen years along with six seasons of only one loss. Carr's great success at the Big House helped his teams win five Big Ten Championships, which is the third best in the legendary history of Michigan football. I don't think that anyone expected Carr to be so successful at Michigan Stadium. It is probably safe to say that Lloyd Carr exceeded all expectations during his tenure in the Big House, except for his own. Go Blue!

CHAPTER 23

A Closer Look:
Lloyd Carr's Michigan Legacy

Lloyd Carr began his head coaching career like no other man in Michigan football history. He was the first, and only, man to be named as the "Interim Head Coach" in Wolverine football history. Carr was also the first, and only, man to take over the Michigan football program in the month of May. Nobody knew how long it would take Mr. Carr to earn the job permanently or be replaced by someone else. As it turned out, he won eight of his first ten games and the "interim" part of his title was removed. Lloyd Carr officially became the "Head Football Coach" at the University of Michigan after his Wolverines defeated Purdue (5-0) on November 11, 1995. Athletic Director Joe Roberson put a lot of faith in Lloyd Carr. I doubt if he really thought about how long Carr would remain at Michigan or how successful he would be. As it turned out, Mr. Roberson made one of the best hiring decisions in the history of Michigan football. Now, it's time to take a final look at Coach Carr's career and document the achievements that made his time in Ann Arbor so special.

When Lloyd Carr retired in January 2008, he had been coaching high school or college football for forty seasons. He left an amazing legacy of personal and professional excellence. Coach Carr is most remembered for winning, a lot of winning. However, his impact at Michigan is far greater than numbers in the "won-lost" columns. First, Lloyd Carr was an exceptional leader, a leader of men, who knew how to bring out the best in his players and coaches. He was also an exemplary role model who showed others how to live and lead with integrity through the power of example. Second, Coach Carr was an exceptional mentor for his coaches and players. He helped his athletes and coaches prepare for successful lives after football. Third, and maybe most importantly, Lloyd H. Carr believed in service. He didn't just talk about doing good. He did some amazing things off the football field that helped countless others in hundreds, or maybe thousands of ways.

A Legacy of Winning at Michigan—the Best Ever!

Yes, Coach Carr's legacy is more than just about winning football games. However, if he wasn't so successful in the "Won-Lost" department, he would not have been around long enough to do everything else that made him so effective for so long. The most important thing that you need to know about Lloyd Carr's legacy is that he is the winningest coach in the history of Michigan football. The chart below shows you why.

Name	Assistant	Wins	Head Coach	Wins	Total-Years/Wins
Carr	1980-1994	134	1995-2007	122	28 years/256 wins
Hanlon	1969-1991	213	N/A	N/A	23 years/213 wins
Keen	1926-1958	196	N/A	N/A	33 years/196 wins
Schembechler	N/A	N/A	1969-1989	194	21 years/194 wins
Oosterbaan	1928-1947	120	1948-1958	63	31 years/183 wins
Yost	N/A	N/A	1901-1926*	165	25 years/165 wins

*Fielding Yost did not coach the 1924 Michigan football team

Coach Carr was an assistant coach for fifteen years for Bo and Mo (10 for Schembechler and 5 for Moeller). Lloyd Carr, and some other talented assistants, helped Bo and Mo win a total of 134 games. (90 for Schembechler and 44 for Moeller). Head Coach Carr won a total of 122 games from 1995 to 2007. When you total all the games that the Wolverines won with Carr on the sidelines as an assistant or head coach the result is 256 victories.

Jerry Hanlon, the second man on this elite list, coached football at Michigan for twenty-three seasons. He was on Bo's staff from 1969 until 1989. He was with Bo for all 194 wins that Schembechler posted in Ann Arbor. Coach Hanlon stayed for the first two years of Gary Moeller's tenure (1990 and 1991). Gary Moeller and his staff added nineteen wins in 1990 and 1991 which raised Hanlon's share of Wolverine wins to 213. That is how Coach Hanlon ended up second on this very impressive list.

Cliff Keen, coached in more football seasons than any other man in Michigan football history (33 seasons). He was on the sidelines to assist five Wolverine head coaches (Fielding Yost, Tad Wieman, Harry Kipke, Fritz Crisler, and Bennie Oosterbaan). Michigan won 196 games when Keen was on the field. Oh, by the way, he is the winningest wrestling coach in Wolverine history. He also has a building named after him on the Michigan campus and founded a very successful business that still carries his name. Yes, Cliff Keen is another Wolverine legend who helped Michigan become the winningest program in college football history.

Bo Schembechler is the winningest head coach in Wolverine football history. His exemplary record at Michigan probably will never be equaled. Bo's 194 wins placed him third in total football coaching victories at Michigan.

Bennie Oosterbaan, Michigan's first three-time All-American, went to work as an assistant coach Tad Wieman after graduation in 1928. He remained as an assistant coach for Harry Kipke and Fritz Crisler. Michigan posted 120 victories during Bennie's "assistant years." Then, he posted 63 wins as Michigan's head football coach from 1948 to 1958. The Wolverines won 183 games when Coach Bennie Oosterbaan roamed the sidelines in Ann Arbor.

Fielding Yost was the head football coach at Michigan for twenty-five years. He set the standard for Wolverine football excellence with 165 wins during his career in Ann Arbor. Only Bo Schembechler has more wins as a head coach.

Yes, Lloyd Carr is at the top of a very short list of Michigan football legends. Thanks to Bo Schembechler and Gary Moeller, Coach Carr became an integral part of the Michigan program. He learned how to contribute to a winning football program. When it was time, he was ready to take charge of Wolverine football and lead it to great heights from 1995 to 2007.

A Legacy of Championships—Twenty-Nine to Be Exact!

Here is something else that you probably didn't know about Lloyd Carr's coaching career in Ann Arbor. As I continued to dig into his career, I learned that Carr had a championship resume that was more impressive than I thought.

When Lloyd Carr ended his amazing career, his name was associated with twenty-nine championships. Yes, Coach Lloyd Carr was around for more trophy case hardware moments than any other coach in Michigan football history. When you compare his contributions to the records of Fielding Yost and Bo Schembechler you understand why Lloyd Carr is at the top of a very distinguished list.

Coach	National Title(s)	Big Ten Titles	Bowl Wins	Total
Carr	1	13	15	29
Schembechler	0	13	5	18
Yost	6	10	1	17

Lloyd Carr is the only man listed above who was both an assistant coach and head coach at Michigan. As a head coach he won a national championship in 1997. As an assistant, he contributed to eight Big Ten Championships (Five for Bo and three for Mo) and won five more Big Ten Titles as a head coach.

That's how he helped the Wolverines earn thirteen conference championships. Coach Carr also helped Michigan win nine bowl game trophies (five with Bo and four with Mo) from 1980 to 1994. Lloyd Carr went on to win six bowl games as a head coach which is why he is associated with fifteen bowl wins. When you total all the numbers, you see that Lloyd Carr's name is associated with twenty-nine trophies that rest in Schembechler Hall. Yes, Lloyd Carr made a very large contribution to the championship legacy of Michigan football.

A Legacy of Consistency!

Lloyd Carr won a lot of games as an assistant coach and head coach. His best season was the 1997 season when his Wolverines posted a perfect record of 12 wins and 0 losses, won a share of the national championship, and won the Big Ten Championship with a perfect record of 8 wins and 0 losses. Of course, some Michigan fans were disappointed that Carr didn't have six or eight more of these perfect seasons. Unfortunately, Lloyd Carr wasn't always perfect but he racked up thirteen straight winning seasons overall. He never had a losing season in the Big Ten play. He had six seasons with ten wins or more. Coach Carr's teams won five Big Ten Championships in his first ten years. Then, things slipped from 2005 to 2007. Overall, the Wolverines were ranked among the top twenty teams (or higher) at end of the season for all but one year (2005) of Coach Carr's tenure.

Here is something else that you need to know about how consistent Lloyd Carr was at Michigan. He coached his Wolverines for forty-four months during thirteen regular seasons. Carr had a winning record in thirty-four of those months and nine months were even. Lloyd Carr only posted one losing month and that was November 2007. He had a record of 1 win and 2 losses in the final month that he coached at Michigan. If you do the math, Coach Carr's Monthly Winning Rate was almost eighty-eight percent (.875). Bottom line—Lloyd H. Carr was a consistent winner!

Believe it or not, it gets better! By the time he hung up his whistle, Lloyd Carr won 122 games in thirteen seasons. That averages out to 9.38 wins per season which is impressive. It is also the best winning rate in Michigan football history. Here is how that winning rate compares to some of the other legends in Wolverine football history who coached for thirteen or more seasons:

Coach	Years at UofM	Total Wins	Average WPS*
Yost	25	165	6.60
Schembechler	21	194	9.23
Carr	13	122	9.38

*Average WPS = Average Wins Per Season

I was absolutely stunned to learn that Coach Lloyd Carr has the highest average wins per season rate in Michigan football history. This information was not common knowledge. It required some digging but I am glad I put these numbers together.

There are a couple of things to remember about these numbers. First, Fielding Yost has the highest winning percentage of any coach in Michigan football history. He won over eighty-three percent (.833) of his games. Scheduling was all over the place in the Yost Years (1901-1926). Coach Yost's first five teams averaged over eleven games per season (11.2). Then, the average number of games dipped to just over six games (6.58) a season from 1906 to 1922. Things moved forward in 1923 and Yost had an average of eight games on his last three schedules. During his twenty-five-year career, Fielding Yost averaged just over eight games per season (8.16). Even with his high winning rate, it was hard for Yost to post a high wins per season rate because he had fewer opportunities.

Bo Schembechler coached for twenty-one years at Michigan. College football was raking in hundreds of hundreds of millions of dollars every season. More games meant more money so college football schedules expanded. Coach Schembechler coached in two-hundred and forty-seven games in twenty-one years. His schedules averaged almost twelve games per season (11.76) including bowl games. Since Bo won about eighty-percent of his games (.795), he became the first Michigan coach to average over nine wins per season (9.23).

Lloyd Carr coached for thirteen seasons, which is less than Fielding Yost or Bo Schembechler. However, he successfully navigated thirteen seasons worth of schedules that included a total of one hundred and sixty-two games. He averaged of twelve games per season (12.46) which gave him numerous opportunities to excel each year. Lloyd Carr's winning rate was just over seventy-five (.753) percent. Yes, Carr had more chances to win more games than any other coach in Wolverine football history. He took advantage of his situation and produced an average of 9.38 wins per season for thirteen years. Lloyd H. Carr is the most consistent winner in Michigan football history—period!

A Legacy of Top Ten Wins!

Yes, everybody wants to beat Michigan. The chart below shows how all Wolverine coaches have fared over the years against some of the tougher competition on their schedules.

Wolverine Coach	Top Ten Record	Top Ten Win %
Crisler	6 wins 7 losses 1 tie	.464
Oosterbaan	9 wins 13 losses 2 ties	.417
Elliott	7 wins 10 losses 0 ties	.412
Schembechler	15 wins 20 losses 1 tie	.431
Moeller	7 wins 5 losses 1 tie	.577
Carr	**18 wins 9 losses**	**.667**
Rodriguez	1 win 4 losses	.200
Hoke	0 wins 4 losses	.000
Harbaugh	5 wins 15 losses	.250
Program Totals	**68-87-5**	**.440**

(Note – The men listed below are the only ones who coached their entire tenure when team rankings were part of college football.)

Once again, Coach Carr's numbers against top ten competition were outstanding. Only Gary Moeller and Lloyd Carr posted winning records against teams that were ranked from #1 to #10. Michigan is almost always the most important game on any opponent's schedule. When you are the winningest team in college football, everybody wants to beat you! It has been that way since the early years of college football and it has been that way for over one hundred years. Carr knew it was that way at Michigan and he embraced the pressure.

Here is a breakdown of the rankings of the teams he faced in the top ten matchups that were on a Michigan football schedule from 1995 to 2007.

Ranking	Games Won	Games Lost
#1	0	2
#2	3	1
#3	1	0
#4	2	0
#5	2	0
#6	1	1
#7	0	2
#8	4	2
#9	3	1
#10	2	0
Totals	18	9

Lloyd Carr is clearly the best coach against top rated teams in Wolverine football history. And it really isn't close. That's all I am going to say about this topic. Coach Carr's record speaks for itself!

A Legacy of Michigan Football Firsts!

Yes, Lloyd Carr won a lot of football games. He also achieved some things in his career that no other Wolverine head coach had ever accomplished. You may remember that Lloyd Carr's first game as Michigan's Head Football Coach ended with seven firsts. Here they are again:

1. Lloyd Carr's first season began in August 1995.
2. Carr's first game was on August 26, 1995.
3. Coach Carr's first game was also the first game that Michigan ever played in the month of August.
4. Carr's first game was also the first time that Michigan played in a nationally televised game called the Kickoff Classic.
5. Lloyd Carr earned his first head coaching victory with a last second win over Virginia (18-17).
6. Coach Carr was the first Michigan coach to lead a team to victory after being down by seventeen-points.
7. Carr's debut was also the first Michigan football game with over fifty passes (52).

Coach Lloyd Carr went on to win a lot more games in the next thirteen years. He also blazed his own trail with many, many more Michigan football "firsts." Here are some more special things that Lloyd Carr achieved during his tenure in Ann Arbor. The next section is focused on what I call "First and Only" or "only" accomplishments.

- Coach Carr is still the only Michigan head coach to win a state championship as a player and a Big Ten Championship along with a national championship as a coach (1997).
- Again, Lloyd Carr is the only Michigan football head coach to be hired in the month of May.
- Lloyd Carr also holds the distinction of being the only "interim" head football coach in Michigan football history.
- Lloyd Carr is the first, and only, Wolverine coach to achieve a final record of 12 wins and 0 losses in one season—so far.
- Carr is the first, and only, Michigan coach to post six bowl game victories.

- Coach Carr is the first, and only, Maize and Blue football coach to win four straight bowl games.
- In 2005, Lloyd Carr became the first, and only, Wolverine football coach to lead a team to two overtime wins in the same month/season.
- Lloyd Carr is the only Michigan coach to have a perfect record in overtime games (5 wins and 0 losses).
- Carr is the first, and only, man to coach a player (Charles Woodson in 1997) who won the Bronco Nagurski, Jim Thorpe, Chuck Bednarik, and Harley Griffin Awards.
- Only one Wolverine player, Chris Perry in 2003, has won the Doak Walker Award and he did it on Lloyd Carr's watch.
- Braylon Edwards is the only Michigan player to win the Fred Bilitnikoff Receiver Award. He also earned that prestigious honor during Lloyd Carr's tenure in 2004.
- Carr is the first, and only, Wolverine coach to post wins in the 100th rivalry game with two rivals (Ohio State 2003 and Michigan State 2007).
- Coach Carr is the only Michigan coach to defeat Notre Dame twice by the same exact score of 38-0.
- Lloyd Carr is the only Head Coach at Michigan to lead a team to 31 points in the final quarter of a football game. (Versus Minnesota in 2003)
- Carr is the only Wolverine head coach to win two overtime road games in the same month and year when his 2005 team defeated Michigan State (34-31) and Iowa (23-20) in October.

Here are some more Michigan football milestones that Lloyd Carr, his coaches, and his players, achieved first.

- Lloyd Carr is the first Michigan Head Coach to have an assistant who won the Broyles Award for the top assistant coach in 1997.
- Coach Carr was the first Michigan coach to win an overtime bowl game when he defeated Alabama (35-34) on January 1, 2000, in the Orange Bowl.
- Carr was also the first Michigan coach to lead his team to an overtime victory in a regular season game. (October 12, 2002, against Penn State (27-24).

- Lloyd Carr was on the Michigan sideline for the 100th anniversary game of the Little Brown Jug series with Minnesota in 2003.
- Coach Carr is the first Michigan coach to coach a player (David Baas in 2004) who won the Dave Rimington Trophy which is awarded to the nation's outstanding offensive center.
- Carr is the only Wolverine head coach to win two overtime games in the same month and year when his 2005 team defeated
- Lloyd Carr is the first Wolverine coach to have a player (LaMarr Woodley in 2006) win the Ted Hendricks Award and the Rotary Lombardi Award.

A Legacy of Service!

Now, it's time to talk about something that Lloyd Carr enjoyed more than winning football games. Coach Carr was even better off the football field than he was on the field.

Image 28: The City of Riverview, Michigan renamed a park in honor of Lloyd Carr in 2008. It was a special way to honor Coach Carr for his dedication to the city and citizens of Riverview. The park is directly across the street from Riverview Community High School. Photo from the Barry Gallagher Family Collection.

Lloyd Henry Carr Jr. set a great example for his players with his passion for giving and serving others. Lloyd Carr started serving and giving back to his community when he was teaching and coaching at the high school level. He was elected to the Riverview Community Schools School Board in 1975 and served a full four-year term. Coach Carr told me in an interview that he learned a lot about leadership and strategic planning during his school board tenure. He also developed a great appreciation for teachers, administrators, and students.

Coach Carr college coaching responsibilities caused him to end his school board service. However, he found ways to use his coaching stature as a platform for many charitable initiatives and service projects.

Here is a sampling of some of the big and little things that Coach Carr did to give back to many good causes in Riverview, Michigan and Ann Arbor, Michigan over the years.

- Coach Carr is blessed to have daughters, daughters-in-law, and granddaughters in his life. Naturally, he felt a need to become a champion for women's sports. He endowed a scholarship at Michigan that is dedicated to a Wolverine woman student-athlete.
- Coach Carr, with the help of some of his coaches and players, made many trips to his hometown of Riverview, Michigan for camps. They helped Carr host his Hall-of-Fame Football Camp to teach the gridiron game to downriver youth. Carr was the driving force in this program for just over thirty years—wow!
- Lloyd Carr created a unique summer fund-raising event called the Women's Football Academy. This popular event helped ladies learn about Michigan Wolverine football and the game of college football. All proceeds from this initiative benefitted the University of Michigan's Comprehensive Cancer Center.
- In 2004, Coach Carr created another fund-raising activity called "Carr's Wash for Kids." Lloyd Carr and his players turned out to wash hundreds of cars in the month of August. All proceeds from this event were directed to C.S. Mott's Children's Hospital.

- Carr, and many of his players, became frequent visitors to Mott hospital. They raised hundreds of sprits and spread a lot of "Maize and Blue" cheer for many years.
- Later, Lloyd Carr served as co-chair of a capital campaign for the new C.S. Mott Children's Hospital. In 2011, the seventh floor of the hospital was named the Coach Carr Pediatric Cancer Center Unit.
- Coach Carr also supported Special Olympics programs in Washtenaw County.
- Carr is a "Concussion Champion" since he actively supports the research programs at the Concussion Center at the University of Michigan Hospital.
- I know that there are many other good causes that received Coach Carr's support over the years. The list that you just read is just a sampling of Lloyd Carr's actions that served his fellow man, and woman, and supported worthy programs in Ann Arbor and the State of Michigan.

Image 29: On October 15, 2022 Lloyd Carr and his football team were honored on the 25th Anniversary of their national championship season in 1997. The University of Michigan also named the legendary Michigan Stadium tunnel after Lloyd Carr. It was quite an honor for Carr who once remarked that the stadium tunnel is "hallowed ground." Photo courtesy of Jeff Spergalas.

A Legacy Worthy of the College Football Hall of Fame!

I always felt that Lloyd Carr was an outstanding coach and leader. Of course, the National Football Foundation agreed since they inducted him into their College Football Hall of Fame in 2011—just four years after his retirement. In case you are not familiar with the criteria for a coach to be inducted into the NFF's Hall of Fame, here is what it takes:

1. Coaches must have at least 10 years of head coaching experience.
2. Coaches must have coached in at least 100 games.
3. Coaches must have at least a sixty-percent (.600), or higher, winning percentage.
4. Football achievements are considered first, but the post-football record as a citizen is also weighed.

Of course, Lloyd Henry Carr Jr. met, and exceeded, every criteria on the NFF's list for Hall of Fame coaches. His impressive coaching credentials allowed him to be elected just four years after he retired. Steve Hatchell, President, and CEO of the National Football Foundation, had this to say about Lloyd Carr's induction into the College Football Hall of Fame: "Lloyd Carr stands among the winningest coaches in college football history." Hatchell continued with, "But, more important is what he stands for and his reputation as a man of integrity with an unequalled passion for mentoring student-athletes who played for him." (National Football Foundation Press Release dated November 11/15/2011, *"Lloyd Carr Set for November 19 NFF Hall of Fame On-Campus Salute."*)

Lloyd Carr's twenty-eight-year coaching journey at the University of Michigan began in 1980 and ended in 2007. He proved himself to be a loyal and effective assistant to Bo Schembechler and Gary Moeller. When Coach Moeller resigned, Carr was given the opportunity of a lifetime. Fortunately, he was the right man at the right time for Michigan. Lloyd Carr really stepped up at a critical time in Wolverine football history and blazed his own trail.

Actually, Coach Carr did more than step up. He excelled at a high level and made his own way in Schembechler Hall. Lloyd Carr took Michigan to a national championship in 1997—the first in five decades. Carr won five Big Ten Championships and finished third in career wins for a Michigan football head coach. Yes, he did pretty good for an "interim" head coach. Now, we call him a "Hall of Famer." Any questions?

Appendix A – Michigan Coaches 1891 to 2022

Coach	Team(s)#	Year(s)	Overall	Win %
Crawford/ Murphy	12	1891	4-5-0	.444
Barbour	13-14	1892-1893	14-8-0	.636
McCauley	15-16	1894-1895	17-2-2	.857
Ward	17	1896	9-1-0	.900
Ferbert	18-20	1897-1898	24-3-1	.875
Lee	21	1900	7-2-1	.750
Yost	22-44	1901-1923	151-27-10	.829
Little	45	1924	6-2-0	.750
Yost	46-47	1925-1926	14-2-0	.875
Wieman	48-49	1927-1928	9-6-1	.593
Kipke	50-58	1929-1937	46-26-4	.631
Crisler	59-68	1938-1947	71-16-3	.805
Oosterbaan	69-79	1948-1958	63-33-4	.650
Elliott	80-89	1959-1968	51-42-2	.547
Schembechler	90-110	1969-1989	194-48-5	.795
Moeller	111-115	1990-1994	44-13-4	.754
Carr	**116-128**	**1995-2007**	**122-40**	**.753**
Rodriguez	129-131	2008-2010	15-22	.405
Hoke	132-135	2011-2014	31-20	.607
Harbaugh	136-143	2015-2022	73-24	.752

Appendix B - Coach Carr's Milestone Victories

Date	Opponent	Score	Milestone
8/26/1995	Virginia	18-17	1st Win
9/02/1995	Illinois	38-14	1st Big Ten Win
10/28/1995	Minnesota	52-17	1st Homecoming Win
11/11/1995	Purdue	5-0	1st Shutout Win
11/01/1997	Minnesota	24-3	25th Victory at UM
11/22/1997	Ohio State	20-14	1st Big Ten Title
01/01/1998	Washington State	21-16	1st Bowl Win
09/19/1998	Eastern Michigan	59-20	Highest Scoring Win
11/07/1998	Penn State	27-0	25th Big Ten Win
09/04/1999	Notre Dame	26-22	50th Win at UM
01/01/2000	Alabama	35-34	1st Overtime Win
09/30/2000	Wisconsin	13-10	800th Wolverine Win
11/16/2002	Wisconsin	21-14	75th Win at UM
10/10/2003	Minnesota	38-35	50th Big Ten Win
10/30/2004	Michigan State	45-37	Only Triple OT Win
10/22/2005	Iowa	23-20	100th Win at UM
09/02/2006	Vanderbilt	27-7	850th Wolverine Win
10/29/2007	Northwestern	28-16	75th Big Ten Win
11/03/2007	Michigan State	28-24	Last Big Ten Win
01/01/2008	Florida	41-35	Last Win (122) at UM

Appendix C - Coach Carr's Honors and Awards

Month/Year	Award/Honor
1962	Michigan High School Football State Champion
1962	All-State Football Team
1975	Michigan HS Regional Coach of the Year
1997	Big Ten Coach of the Year
1997	Bear Bryant Coach of the Year
1997	Walter Camp Coach of the Year
1997	Catholic League Hall of Fame
1997	Northern Michigan University Hall of Fame
2004	Jewish Sports Hall of Fame
2007	Bobby Dodd Coach of the Year
2007	Honorary PhD – University of Michigan
2007	Park in Riverview, Michigan Named After Lloyd Carr
2008	Honorary PhD – Albion College
2011	Michigan Sports Hall of Fame
2011	National Football Foundation Hall of Fame
2013	Rose Bowl Hall of Fame
2015	University of Michigan Athletic Hall of Honor
2021	Kappa Sigma Fraternity Co-Man of the Year
2021	Orange Bowl Hall of Fame
2022	Lloyd Carr Tunnel Dedication at Michigan Stadium

Appendix D - Coach Carr's Monthly Record

Year	August	September	October	November	December	January	Total
1995	1-0	4-0	2-1	2-2	0-1	N/A	9-4
1996	1-0	3-0	2-1	2-2	N/A	0-1	8-4
1997	N/A	3-0	4-0	4-0	N/A	1-0	12-0
1998	N/A	2-2	4-0	3-1	N/A	1-0	10-3
1999	N/A	4-0	2-2	3-0	N/A	1-0	10-2
2000	N/A	4-1	2-2	2-0	N/A	1-0	9-3
2001	N/A	3-1	3-0	2-2	N/A	0-1	8-4
2002	1-0	3-1	2-1	3-1	1-0	N/A	10-3
2003	1-0	3-1	3-1	3-1	N/A	0-1	10-3
2004	N/A	3-1	5-0	1-1	N/A	0-1	9-3
2005	N/A	2-2	4-1	1-1	0-1	N/A	7-5
2006	N/A	5-0	4-0	2-1	N/A	0-1	11-2
2007	N/A	3-2	4-0	1-2	N/A	1-0	9-4
Totals	4-0	42-11	41-9	29-14	1-2	5-5	122-40

Appendix E – Riverview High School Football Legends

Before we leave Riverview, here is an incredible insight into the impact that Riverview football and the Pirate coaches have had on college and professional football. I think that Riverview High School is the only school in America that has produced three NCAA College Football National Championship alumni and another one who earned four NFL Super Bowl Rings. (I apologize for the glare on this image, we couldn't find anyone to block the sun, close the windows, or open the trophy case to get a better picture.)

Image 30: Riverview High School may be the only high school to claim four alumni who earned four Super Bowl Championships and three NCAA national championships in football. From left to right, I will connect each helmet with the Pirate who donated the headgear to the RHS trophy case. Photo from the Barry Gallagher Family Collection.

Robert "Woody" Widenhofer was born in Butler, Pennsylvania and spent his boyhood years in Pennsylvania. He attended Riverview High School from 1957 to 1961 and played on the Pirate football team. He went to the University of Missouri where he played linebacker from 1961 to 1964. After graduation, Woody began his coaching career at Michigan State University as a defensive line coach. He also coached linebackers at Eastern Michigan and Minnesota.

Widenhofer landed a job as a linebacker coach for the Pittsburgh Steelers in 1973. He was promoted to defensive coordinator in 1979. During his time in Pittsburgh, the Steelers won four Super Bowl Championships. Woody only donated one helmet, but he has four special rings. Yes, he had quite a run with Chuck Noll in Pittsburgh.

The second helmet on the left is from the University of Alabama. Mike Vollmar is another former Pirate football player who enjoyed a successful career in college football but not as a coach. Mike graduated from Sienna Heights University in 1988. He was a pole vaulter who majored in history and minored in speech communications. Mike earned a master's degree in sport management. Vollmar worked in athletic administration and recruiting operations at Michigan, Syracuse, and Michigan State. In 2008 Vollmar was hired by Nick Saban to director football operations at Alabama. The Alabama helmet is from the Crimson Tide's 2009 national championship team.

Of course, the iconic Michigan Wolverine helmet was donated by Lloyd H. Carr Jr. after he and his beloved team won the national championship in 1997. As I already mentioned, Coach Carr also attended the University of Missouri before finishing his education and his football career at Northern Michigan University. He enjoyed a successful thirteen year career as the head football coach at Michigan,

The "Buffs" helmet is the last helmet on the right. That helmet was donated by Bill McCartney who graduated from RHS in 1958. McCartney also played college football at the University of Missouri. After graduation, he coached high school football in the Detroit area from 1965 until 1973. In 1974, McCartney became the first, and only, coach that Bo Schembechler ever hired directly from a high school coaching position. He worked for Bo until 1982 when he became the Head Coach at the University of Colorado. McCartney had a successful thirteen-year tenure at Colorado. He led the Buffaloes to the national championship (shared with Georgia Tech) in 1990 and also claimed three Big Eight Conference football championships.

That is just the tip of the iceberg about the great history of the Riverview Pirate football program. I am sure that someone could write a good book about is someday.

Bibliography

Borton, John and Paul Dodd. *Wolverines Handbook: Stories, Stats and Stuff About Michigan Football.* Wichita: The Wichita Eagle and Beacon Publishing Company, 1996

Boyles, Bob, and Paul Guido. *The USA Today College Football Encyclopedia.* New York: Sky Horse Publishing, 2011

Changelis, Angelique. *100 Things Michigan Fans Should Know and Do Before They Die.* Chicago: Triumph Books, 2009.

Cromartie, Bill. *The Big One: Michigan vs. Ohio State.* Nashville, TN: Rutledge Hill Press, 1989.

Emmanuel, Greg. *The 100-Yard War: Inside the 100-Year-Old Michigan-Ohio State Football Rivalry.* Hoboken, NJ: John Wiley and Sons, 2004.

Gallagher, Barry. *The Nasty Football History of Michigan vs. Michigan State 1898 to 2021.* Aurora, Illinois: Power Group Publishing, 2021.

Gallagher, Barry. *The Greatest Football Story Ever Told: Michigan vs. Ohio State 1897-2022.* Aurora, Illinois: Power Group Publishing, 2021.

Geelhoed, E. Bruce. *Bump Elliott, the Michigan Wolverines and Their 1964 Championship Football Season.* Jefferson, NC: McFarland & Company, Inc., Publishers, 2014

Green, Jerry. *The University of Michigan Football Vault: The History of the Wolverines.* Atlanta: Whitman Publishing, LLC, 2008

Kryk, John. *Natural Enemies: Major College Football/s Oldest, Fiercest Rivalry—Michigan vs. Notre Dame.* New York: Taylor Trade Publishing, 2007.

Madej, Bruce with Greg Kinney, Mike Pearson, and Rob Toonkel. *Michigan: Champions of the West.* Champaign: Sports Publishing, 1997.

Magee, Ken and Jon M. Stevens. *The Game: The Michigan-Ohio State Football Rivalry.* Charleston, SC: Arcadia Publishing, 2015.

Michigan Daily. *Michigan Football: From the Pages of the Michigan Daily.* Chicago: Triumph Books, 2012.

Perry, Will. *The Wolverines: The Story of Michigan Football.* Huntsville, AL: Strode Publishing, 1974.

Acknowledgements

Appreciation and gratitude are important parts of the book publishing process. This book is no exception. First, I thank God for my life and I thank God for my wife. My beloved wife Carol is the most important person in my life. I could not have written this book without her constant love and support. She is the most understanding and loving person I know. I am so fortunate to have shared the best portion of my life with this amazing woman. She always keeps me grounded and has always supported me in my work. Thank you, my darling!

Second, I am so blessed to have the love and support of our five children. Even though I have fathered Army Mules, Spartans, Broncos, and Xavier Musketeers, they still love me even though I love the Michigan Wolverines! Thank you, Mike, Mark, Wendy, Marty, and Matthew! I love you and your families so much.

Third, I am grateful to Michigan Man Rich Hewlett for his support of this book and for his amazing Foreword. I have been fortunate to know Rich for the last ten years. We don't speak that often but he is always there for me when I need something related to Wolverine football. I knew that Rich enjoyed a special relationship with Coach Carr. Their friendship has endured and deepened for over forty-years. No one could have written a better "setting" for this book. Thank you Rich!

Fourth, thank you to Chuck Romano for his great work on the book cover. I am so blessed to know him and constantly benefit from his creative talents. I am also indebted to Tracy Atkins from Book Design Templates for all the outstanding work on the interior design of this book. Thank you Chuck and Tracy for your contributions to this book!

Fifth I am grateful to the Bentley Historical Library at The University of Michigan. The Bentley Library is an amazing repository of the history of The University of Michigan. The incredible collection of football records and documents helped me greatly in researching and writing his book. Greg Kinney, Sarah McLusky, and Caitlin Moriarty helped me at every turn. Thank you Greg, Sarah, and Caitlin—you are absolutely the best at what you do!

Sixth, I also wish to recognize the work of legendary Michigan photographer Bob Kalmbach who donated thousands of photographs to the Bentley Historical Library. His pictures are timeless and I am grateful to include many of his outstanding images in this book. Thank you to Bob Kalmbach for a lifetime of Wolverine sports photography excellence! May Bob Kalmbach Rest In Peace!

Seventh, I want to thank Sara Stillman, another talented photographer for the images that she donated to the Bentley Historical Library. Sara was a photographer for The Michigan Daily in the late 1990s. She took some amazing pictures of Michigan's national championship season in 1997. Thank you Sara for allowing Wolverine football fans to enjoy her outstanding work.

Eighth, I am so grateful for the help of two sports information department professionals from Northern Michigan University (Zach Nicholas) and Eastern Michigan University (Greg Steiner). They searched the archives at both schools and came up with some great pictures that really helped me tell the early part of Lloyd Carr's story. Thank you Zach and Greg!

Ninth, I always take time to thank my high school Creative Writing teacher, Mr. Richard Hill. He taught me some important things about writing that I still practice today. Most importantly, he instilled a passion for writing that I carry with me over fifty-years later! Mr. Hill is also a die-hard Michigan Wolverine Fan and proud graduate of the University of Michigan. Thank you, Mr. Hill and Go Blue!

Tenth, although there was no single book that documented the complete history of The University of Michigan football program, there is plenty of information available. I am grateful to all the authors I have cited in my bibliography. I enjoyed reading their books and appreciate their contributions to the amazing story of the Maize and Blue football team. Thank you, authors and journalists!

Eleventh, I am so fortunate to have met one of Lloyd Carr's very good friends named Jeff Spergalas. They share a passion for Riverview, Michigan, a passion for football, a passion for teaching, and a passion for coaching. Jeff agreed to meet with me prior to the publication of this book. He gave me a tour of Riverview High School and took me on a guided tour of the City of Riverview. He even showed me some of the houses that Coach Carr lived in as a boy and later as a resident. He also loaned me some yearbooks and shared some of the photographs that are used in this book. This book is so much better because of Jeff's efforts and support. Thank you Jeff for everything you did to help me share Coach Carr's love of Riverview and for Riverview's love of Coach Carr.

Finally, thanks to Coach Carr for meeting with me and supporting this project. Over ninety-five percent of this book was completed before I met with him.

I had a "proof copy" of the book to show him and he was genuinely excited about my work. He really liked the cover and the book description on the back of the book. So, we were off to a good start. Of course, meeting with Coach Carr only validated my desire to tell his story. Thank you Coach Lloyd Carr for being a legendary football coach and a better man. You are a credit to your family, the City of Riverview, the University of Michigan, and college football. Go Pirates and Go Blue!

Photo Courtesy of Mike Tanner, Saint Mike's Photography

About the Author

Barry Gallagher is a proud graduate of Romeo High School in Romeo, Michigan. He was also fortunate to graduate from Eastern Michigan University where he earned a bachelor's degree in Secondary Education and a master's degree in educational administration. From 1973 to 1983 he worked as a teacher, coach, school administrator, and served in the U. S. Army Reserve. In 1983 he went on active duty and served in various positions as a Military Police Officer and Human Resources Officer. Gallagher retired as a Colonel in 2003. Barry is the author of four books on Michigan Wolverine football and five other books.

If you enjoyed this book, it would be great if you could leave a positive review on Amazon. It is amazingly easy to do, and I would really appreciate it. Thank You!

Other Books by Barry Gallagher:

- *How to Get a Kick Out of Coaching Youth Soccer*

- *The Secrets of Life Power*

- *Michigan Football's Greatest Era*

- *The Legend of Bo Schembechler*

- *Teacher STRONG:-Daily Quotes to Inspire America's Teachers*

- *Leader STRONG: Daily Quotes to Inspire Leaders Everywhere*

- *The Nasty Football History of Michigan and Michigan State – 1898 to 2021*

- *The Greatest Football Story Ever Told: Michigan vs. Ohio State – 1897 to 2022*

- *Choices Matter-Everyday!*

How to contact Barry Gallagher:

E-Mail: powergroup@comcast.net or bbgallagher@comcast.net

Website: www.gobluefootballhistorian.com

Made in the USA
Monee, IL
03 September 2023